Walk in 'e Moon

TO: MY FRIEND JDITH (J.R.)
RICHMUND

Walk in 'e Moon

By LaVerne Thornton

Illustrations by Perry Harrison

CHAPEL HILL
PRESS, INC.

Illustrations by Perry Harrison

ISBN 978-1-59715-067-5
Library of Congress Catalog Number 2010926143

First Printing

In memory of
Mama, whose wisdom and love
shaped the boy I was and the man I became,
and
Dave, my best friend for more than twenty years,
whose last days were made easier when
his family read him my stories.

Contents

Acknowledgments ix

Foreword xi

Paths Much Traveled 1

Shotgun Essie 7

Uncle Luther and Aunt Duddy 10

Missing Pieces 13

Whistle Britches, Nutcracker, and Pee Wee 15

First Bicycle 18

Tire Ups and Downs 22

The Great Scarf Episode 25

School Lunches 29

Claustrophobia 31

The Disappearing Pocketbooks 35

My Permanent Record 38

Turning Twelve 42

Summer of Discontent 48

Skinny-Dipping 53

How about Them Apples 59

Tall Cotton Silk Stilts 64

The Fart Heard All over Pittsylvania County 67

Sex in the Bend 69

Sowing Wild Oats 75

Hermon's First Time 80

Calling Time 83

Breaking Out 89

A Boy Named LaVerne? 94

Feed-Sack Fashions 97

Lye Soap 101

Wash Day 104

Whitewash 108

Waste Not 113

Southern Revivals 117

The Poorhouse 122

Low-Hanging Fruit 125

Kisses and Fried Apple Pies 128

Putting Food on the Table 133

Milking Cows 139

Making Molasses 144

Strange Edibles 147

Planting Tobacco and Pilot Mountain 155

Mules Cause Cussing 159

Idle Hands 164

Sibling Camaraderie 166

Taught by Adages and Proverbs 173

As the Twig Is Bent, So Grows the Tree 179

Walk in 'e Moon 186

Acknowledgments

To my family, who have heard some of my stories over and over, but have listened patiently. However, I have often caught sight of rolling eyes and a whispered, "Daddy told us that one before." Now—Lucille, LaVisa, and Perry—each of you has some tales that you can read over and over to yourself. I know that you just can't get enough of my stories. To our son, Perry, I offer a special thank-you for gently persuading me to write this book.

To Perry Harrison, a retired Chatham County Schools superintendent in North Carolina, who grew up on a farm just as I did and had similar experiences. I tell and write my stories; he draws authentic depictions of what he hears and sees from my words and his memories. I have known and admired Perry for years since serving with him on a biracial committee that addressed school integration issues in the 1960s. I wrote a story about how one of my schoolteachers, Clarence Shipton, provided me a breakout moment in my life. I gave it to my friend Rob Tharp, a retired Chatham County Schools principal, to read. After reading that story, Rob asked me to let him read some more of my stories. Then Rob suggested that I ask Perry Harrison to illustrate my book. I met with Perry. His wonderful illustrations in this book tell the rest of the story.

To Dee Utley, a retired Moore County Schools teacher, who edited spelling and punctuation errors. She came to our home and worked on my computer to edit. Lucille and I provided lunch on those days, and we developed a lifelong friendship with Dee.

To Neil MacDonald, a retired Lee County Schools principal and schoolteacher, who did the final editing, including what I call the fit-and-finish editing. I met Neil about seven years ago at the St. Luke United Methodist Church Wednesday morning prayer breakfast in Sanford, North Carolina. Neil is a fine man, but my goodness, what a nitpicker. I should have known better than to get a retired schoolteacher and principal to edit my stories. Many of the stories depict my giving teachers and principals a hard time in grammar school. I really believe that Neil felt obligated to get even with me on behalf of all the past teachers and principals upon whom I brought grief. From the day I gave Neil my stories until he mercifully completed his work, I feel that I have been sent to stand in the corner of the room innumerable times.

To Lora Wright, who convinced me that my stories have broad appeal. I knew Lora only casually until we had a delightful conversation one day in Southern Jewelers, her store in Sanford, North Carolina. She asked me where and how I grew up. At some point in the conversation, I told her that I was writing stories about the unique lifestyle and culture in which I was raised. She insisted that I let her read some of my stories. Well, one story led to another one and another one, until she was reading every story I wrote as I wrote them. Lora, you either loved my stories, or you are a most beautiful, sweet liar.

To the staff at Virlie's Grill located at 58 Hillsboro Street in Pittsboro, North Carolina. Aside from Virlie's being an excellent place to eat homemade food, owners Chris and Megan Pratt and the good people of Virlie's generously allowed Perry, me, and later on Neil to conduct our editing and illustration meetings there. We three old men created quite a stir as many of the regulars learned that all the paper shuffling, sketching on napkins, laughter, and animated conversations were about a book on which we were working entitled *Walk in 'e Moon*.

The following conversation is typical of many that we had: Neil would ask, "Now, LaVerne, looking into the face of the cow, on which side of the cow did you sit to milk?" "On the left," I replied. "Well, Perry, you need to change your illustration and put LaVerne on the correct side." I was about to say, "Oh no, no, Perry has it right," but Neil quickly added, "LaVerne wrote in the story that the cow first kicked the bucket over, then slapped his face with her cocklebur-laden tail, and finally peed on the hard, dirt, barn floor, spattering him and the milk pail. As LaVerne ran crying to the house, he left the cow eating grain with a grin on her big, fat, bitchy cow lips. Perry, your illustration shows a very pleasant cow. Can you draw the cow that LaVerne described?"

Perry would begin sketching the "mad cow" on a napkin before Neil finished talking and then ask me for more details. Perry was always willing and wanting to depict the characters and settings as authentically as possible.

Throughout months of such meetings, the staff kept three hungry men fed and content. Our sincere thanks go out to all the fine folks at Virlie's.

Foreword

A few miles northeast of Eden, North Carolina, the Dan River crosses the North Carolina state line and passes under a camelback bridge into Virginia. One half of the bridge is in North Carolina, and one half is in Virginia. About one mile northeast of the bridge, the river is fully in Virginia. The Dan River wiggles northeasterly for several miles, then bends south, back into North Carolina. The river then takes a hairpin turn into Danville, Virginia. As the river flows into Virginia and back into North Carolina, it carves out a several-thousand-acre parcel of Virginia, leaving a deep, bend-shaped, landlocked area of the Old Dominion State. The people, including my family, living in the area were referred to as the Bend People. The unique hairpin turn back into Danville would have required that two bridges be built in order to accommodate the few people living in the Bend. The Bend was northeast of Eden, North Carolina, and was truly, in so many ways, like God's beautiful, isolated Garden of Eden.

The Bend was settled early in America's history by land-grant settlers. About thirty families remained there while I was growing up. We were largely ignored or unknown by Virginia and not totally accepted by North Carolina. The power lines, telephone lines, newspaper delivery, and even the U.S. mail stopped at the last house in North Carolina on Gravel Hill Road. I never saw a Virginia law enforcement officer come to the Bend for the entire eighteen years that I lived there. We were fortunate in that we only had to walk one-half mile to get our newspaper, mail, and the *Progressive Farmer* magazine. Others in the Bend had to travel as much as two miles for their mail. We were several miles from the nearest paved road.

Then and even today, there was only one road, Gravel Hill Road, that left North Carolina and went eight-tenths of a mile into the Bend. The houses did not line up neatly along this short road but were tucked back in the woods at the end of wagon roads or paths. As automobiles became more prevalent in the 1940s, driveways were improved to accept them. Getting stuck in mud remained a common occurrence in the Bend until I went away to college. Paths crisscrossed the entire area connecting all the homes in the Bend and led to swimming and fishing holes in the Dan River. Just about everyone fished and hunted.

Almost everyone in the Bend also raised tobacco. Some farmers raised a little tobacco and also worked at Dan River Mills, a cotton mill. The people who worked in the mill were called the "gray people" due to their pale appearances from working in the sweatshops and their lack of farmers' tans in the summer. Until about 1950, when tractors were introduced in the Bend, farming was done with mule- and horse-drawn implements.

Most of our food was raised on the land, both meat and vegetables. Store-bought items consisted mainly of salt, pepper, coffee, and some spices. Occasionally a family would treat itself to something special like salt herring bought from a wooden barrel at Mr. Walter Smart's country store across the state line in North Carolina. Farmers carried accounts at Mr. Smart's store, which were settled in the fall when tobacco was sold. There was not a single commercial operation in the Bend.

I grew up in the Bend, the only son of my mother, Ethel May Pruitt Thornton, and my dad, Perry James Thornton, along with my three sisters—Betty Jean, Elaine, and Brenda. My maternal grandmother, Essie, who came to be known as "Shotgun Essie," lived alone across the hollow from us. Having survived the Great Depression, known to my parents as "Hoover Days," my father was determined to be as self-reliant as possible. He possessed all the skills necessary to live off the land. He never liked electricity, and 'til the day he died he felt it improper to pee in the house. Between Mama and Daddy's skills, we had a great quality and variety of food. We grew enough food to share with our less fortunate relatives and others living in the city. By this and other acts, my parents instilled in us kids a concern for other people. Having survived the Great Depression, my dad felt that the closer you could come to living off the land, the better off you were.

The Bend People were strong, resilient, and self-reliant. They were tempered by the Great Depression and by living half the 1940s embroiled in World War II. They gathered at Hickory Grove, a small Methodist church across the state line in North Carolina, to share fellowship, celebrate each other's joyous occasions, and comfort one another during their times of suffering. I don't believe that a single wealthy person lived in the Bend. The people were uniformly poor and had a homogenous lifestyle and culture. We kids would often stay overnight with one another. We could go to sleep in one house, awaken in another, and never sense a difference in lifestyle. Every house had a cast-iron pot mounted on bricks or stones in the backyard used for boiling clothes, making lye soap and lard, and making hominy and Brunswick stew. There was a large bell mounted on a post used only for ringing in emergencies. No one in the Bend had grassy yards. They were kept swept clean with brush brooms made from dogwood saplings.

While growing up, I never realized just how unique my home and life were until I had been away for years. I left the Bend to pursue a degree in engineering at Virginia Tech in the fall of

1955. As far as I know, during that time I was the first person from the area to go to college. My body left, but my heart and soul never quite disconnected from the Bend.

I would frequently relate some story to our children and friends that would come across as hard to believe. I was often told, "You should write some of this stuff down." Well, I have started to write short stories of this place and time that I hope will give glimpses into a unique lifestyle and a lost culture.

The following maps show the locations of the Bend; some cities, roads, rivers, and special places; and the houses of some people mentioned in the stories.

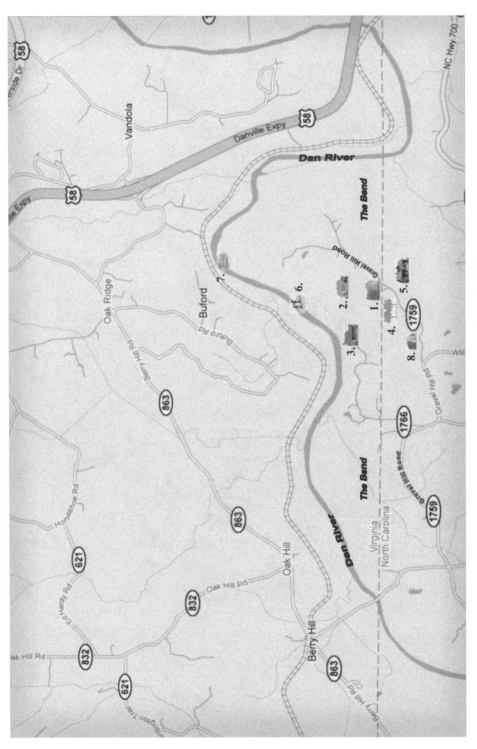

1. LaVerne's House
2. Shotgun Essie's House
3. Uncle Zack and Aunt Jenny's House
4. Lacy Graham's Apple Orchard

5. Janey Dix's House
6. "Turning Twelve" Inspiration Spot
7. "Skinny-Dipping" Swimming Hole
8. Doochie's Barn

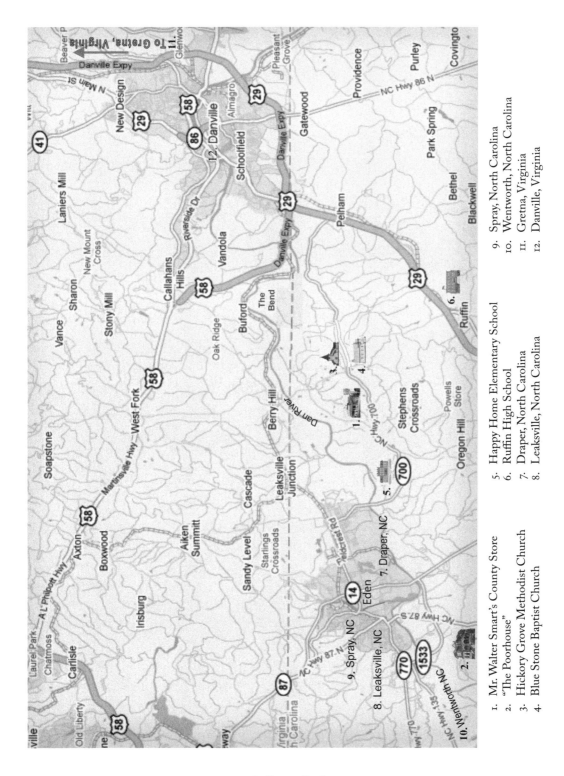

1. Mr. Walter Smart's County Store
2. "The Poorhouse"
3. Hickory Grove Methodist Church
4. Blue Stone Baptist Church
5. Happy Home Elementary School
6. Ruffin High School
7. Draper, North Carolina
8. Leaksville, North Carolina
9. Spray, North Carolina
10. Wentworth, North Carolina
11. Gretna, Virginia
12. Danville, Virginia

Paths Much Traveled

We have all heard and used the word "path" metaphorically—path to destruction, headed on a path to success, going down the wrong path, and so on. Where I grew up in the Bend, paths were real things that took real people to real folks' homes. Some of the houses in the Bend were built before there were roads. Those houses were usually built by or near springs that served as a family's water supply. Paths connected nearly all the homes in the Bend. When roads were built, they were dirt and weren't even covered with a good layer of stone. You either walked in sticky red mud that would build up on your feet in wet weather, or get drenched in dust by a passing automobile in dry weather. Paths provided a clean walk through beautiful forests and winding creeks. They would divert by springs so a person's thirst could be quenched if needed. There was usually a gourd dipper welcoming you to the family spring. These springs offered a variety of tastes depending on the type of trees surrounding them. Poplar trees gave a different flavor than did sycamore or oak trees. With no phones, local newspapers, or any other form of communication except neighbor to neighbor by word of mouth, news about families was most often delivered by someone in person on paths much traveled and relayed around the Bend. When visiting a neighbor, one might run into a friend on the path, sit on a log, and talk for awhile—not that it mattered, because the people you were to visit probably did not know that you were coming anyway.

Most people had a large bell mounted on a post. This bell was to be rung only in an emergency. If a bell was rung several times, neighbors could tell by the sound's direction which neighbor was in distress. A ringing bell meant neighbors would be coming up the path to lend a helping hand. We kids were warned to never ring the bell except for real emergencies. Can't you just imagine? These bells were to us kids what lawyers call "an attractive nuisance." It was posted there with a rope hanging from it, just waiting to be tugged. Communication to one's family members out working in the fields was by hollering your own distinct holler: "Dinner time!" "Company is here!"

My granny, Shotgun Essie, told me a lot about the history of the Bend. Granny married my grandfather, Charlie Pruitt. Grandfather Charlie died before I was born. Grandfather Charlie's

great-grandfather was nicknamed "Walking Bob" Pruitt. Walking Bob was of Irish descent and was married to a woman of Irish descent. Through a land grant they acquired a portion of land bordering the Dan River in the heart of what became known as the Bend. Their reason for settling so deep into the woods was to have proximity to a spring branch with a good downhill flow. The location was ideal for making whiskey. Being of Irish descent, my great-great-grandparents were born with whiskey making in their blood. They contracted with the government to operate a whiskey still. With money from operating the still and some smarts, Bob Pruitt accumulated several thousand acres of land on up the river into North Carolina. His habit of constantly walking his land earned him the nickname "Walking Bob" Pruitt.

His two sons inherited the land. My great-granddaddy was known as "Fiddling Bob" Pruitt, nicknamed for his habit of sitting in a rowboat in the middle of the Dan River drinking and fiddling. When he ran out of money, he would sell some land. What he did was fiddle and drink away my side of the family's wealth. His brother developed and enhanced his wealth. He was involved in starting and investing in several successful businesses in the Danville, Virginia, area, including Smith Douglas Fertilizer Company, American National Bank, and a number of tobacco sales houses.

The still was in operation when my granny was a little girl. She tells a story about how people would bring their own bottles to the still to have them filled right out of the vat, using a gourd dipper and a funnel. She told about working as a little girl bringing firewood to the still. Granny said that at one time all paths led to Walking Bob's still. I suppose it was similar to today's modern airline hub. I loved for her to tell stories about the still. She told me a story about a regular who came once wearing a long, heavy overcoat. He pulled his bottle from the overcoat lining and had it filled. Once the bottle was filled, he shoved it back into his coat and said, "I will pay you next week." The policy was "absolutely no credit." When it was commanded that he return the whiskey, he cursed, jerked the bottle out, and commenced to pour the whiskey back into the vat. Walking Bob grabbed the bottle and tasted the contents. It was water. A search revealed that he had been carrying two bottles in his overcoat lining—one empty and one full of water. His intention was to pull a clever switch.

I was eight years old when World War II ended. The impact on me was such that I remember much about the war. Two of my uncles, Granny Essie's sons, were in the war. Uncle Wallace Pruitt saw rough action, having been with the follow-up troops behind D-Day, and having participated in the Battle of the Bulge. One of the paths much traveled in the Bend went from Granny's house to Uncle Zack and Aunt Jenny's house. They were a black couple who were my family's good friends. Aunt Jenny and Uncle Zack had a son in the war also. Aunt Jenny couldn't read, so many afternoons after the *Danville Register and Bee* newspaper arrived,

she would walk the path to Granny's house. I remember that, on most summer days, Granny and Aunt Jenny would sit under a big oak tree in Granny's yard, and Granny would read the paper to Aunt Jenny. They would often cry together. This affected me because I really didn't understand enough to sort it all out in my young brain. I knew it was something bad, and I knew that Japs and Germans must be bad people.

It took years for my fear of and dislike for the Germans and Japanese to fade away. When I was about thirty-five years old, I visited an industrial plant in Germany. No one in the reception area spoke English. They were expecting me, so they took me to a room to wait for the plant manager. The room had only a wooden table surrounded by eight straight-back chairs. There were no other adornments. I waited about twenty minutes for the plant manager to arrive. During that time, I reflected on the war and the big difference between my visit and my Uncle

Wallace's time there. Suddenly the door opened, and in walked a light blond-haired man with pale blue eyes. He looked ten feet tall and was the very epitome of the Aryan man that I had imagined. For a moment the hair on the back of my neck stood up. My voice cracked when I spoke. Fortunately, I was treated so well by the German people that all animosity toward them disappeared. I haven't been to Japan.

I can still see Aunt Jenny walking up the path to Granny's house in her bonnet and apron with a snuff brush in her mouth. Women during that era did not want to tan; it would show that they were poor farm folks. Therefore, most women in the Bend wore homemade bonnets with wide brims to shade their entire faces. They wore long sleeves and long skirts. Sometimes they wore gloves when working outside.

Many women dipped snuff, but I don't recall ever seeing a woman smoking. A sourwood stick about one-quarter inch in diameter and about four or five inches long was used to dip snuff. The stick was chewed on one end until it became sort of fuzzy. It was moistened with spittle dipped in the snuff box and inserted into the bottom lip. Aunt Jenny and Granny would sit for hours with Granny reading, both dipping, and both crying over their loved ones at war. How could a child forget this scene? Uncle Zack for some reason called me Tutter. By today's standards, he died fairly young. I didn't understand death, but I knew it hurt really badly. I missed walking that path to visit Uncle Zack and Aunt Jenny.

Those old, much-traveled paths existed and were used during my youth. They are mostly gone now. A few remain and are used by deer hunters. Most all of the houses, built well away from the one road there, have rotted and fallen down. A few houses have been built since I left the Bend in 1955. All were built along the still lone road that always served the Bend. Just about all the kids of my generation left for very different lives. I can't bring myself to say "better lives."

Shotgun Essie

Grandmothers are great. They will allow you more freedom than parents will, and they are not as uptight about words. My grandmother Essie on my mother's side lived alone from my earliest memories. There was a path leading from our house down the hollow to the spring where we got our water. A path ran up the other side of the hollow to my grandmother's house. For several years when I was in grammar school, I would have supper at my house and then go to Granny's to stay overnight. Granny would spend days without speaking with an adult. This caused her to talk with me sometimes as if I were an adult. Granny told me one night about a neighbor woman being pregnant. This was a time when boys were old enough to impregnate a girl long before they had heard that word. In those days a woman was "in the family way." On one occasion I came home and announced to my mother that I had heard that Mrs. Hazelwood was pregnant. I thought my mother was going to faint. This stopped me from revealing to my mother Granny's conversations with me.

One day at Mr. Walter Smart's store, a man asked Mr. Smart, "Who is that little boy?"

Mr. Smart said, "That is Shotgun Essie's grandboy."

I could hardly wait to get to Granny's house that night. As soon as I could work it into our conversation, I told Granny about the man at the store and what he had asked Mr. Smart. I asked her why Mr. Smart called her Shotgun Essie. Granny told me that Granddaddy Charlie died from a heart attack when he was forty-five years old. Granny said that she was pregnant with her sixth child at the time. (She said that word to me again.) Soon after his death the baby was born, but the stress of it all brought on childbirth insanity. She was totally out of it for more than a year—crazy as a bedbug, she said. Nowadays they call it postpartum depression. In the meantime, my then eighteen-year-old mother, the oldest of six children, had to look after Grandmother and five younger brothers and sisters. There were no so-called social services available at the time. The three oldest were very pretty girls ranging in age from fourteen to eighteen. The young men in the area started to sexually harass the girls. (See, another forbidden word from my granny.) One day Granny sat up in bed and asked, "Where is Charlie?" It was,

she said, as if she never knew Granddaddy had died. From that day forward, Granny was an extremely strong woman. She took no crap from anyone.

One day, three men, thinking that Granny was still crazy, came around to try to take advantage of my mother and her sisters. Granny came out and ordered them to leave. They got ugly, so Granny went into the house and came back with her shotgun. When the men turned to run, Granny said (and these are her own words), "I shot one of the bastards in the ass." From that day forward, men would approach Granny's house in a prayer posture. I could not wait to get to school the next day and tell Granny's story. She had a reputation already because of discussing the "pregnant" word with me.

When my schoolmates heard that Granny used the "bastard" and "ass" words, her reputation grew. Some of the boys, who had never met Granny, claimed to have discussed sex, history, politics, religion, and so forth with her. By the end of the school day I had told that story over and over. The "bastard" and "ass" words had started to roll off my tongue as easily as quoting John 3:16 in Sunday school.

As I write my memories of growing up, you will read a great deal about my granny. She influenced my life in ways that I only became aware of as my own life unfolded with time.

My attention was caught once by a cartoon showing a winter living-room scene. A fire was burning in the fireplace, and a little boy was lying on the floor looking up at a gray-haired granny. The granny, who was rocking and knitting, had on a high-necked black dress with a white lace collar, and her hair was pulled back in a bun. I was in my thirties and had not thought of my granny as often as I should have. My eyes welled up as memories of such evenings with my granny flooded over me. Then I read the caption. The little boy said, "Granny, tell me again about the time you was a whore in Chicago."

Tears rolled from my eyes with laughter. I thought, *Granny, you got another one on me from your grave.*

Uncle Luther and Aunt Duddy

If there ever were two married people whom one could describe as "real pieces of work," my Uncle Luther and Aunt Duddy would have to be included. Each was a real piece of work in his or her own right, but collectively they were an outstanding piece of work! Aunt Duddy was my mother's sister, and Uncle Luther was my dad's brother. They lived a long walking distance from us and had a son one year older than I was. I had plenty of time to be involved in their lives. In the 1940s, parents were not concerned about kids leaving home alone to wander about the countryside. We had a large amount of freedom in the Bend, but Aunt Duddy was the most lenient of all the parents. I went to Aunt Duddy's house one day by myself to play with my cousin, and Aunt Duddy told me, "I don't know where Larry went; he took food so he may be gone a few days." Larry was six and I was five at the time. Luther and Duddy loved some, drank some, and fought quite a bit. Their call to fame with me was creative cussing. Those two elevated cussing to an art form.

I remember one day that Larry and I were shooting marbles in his yard. We could draw a marble shooting ring anywhere in our yards. No one had grass. We all had clean dirt yards—grass and weed free. Instead of mowing grass, we kids had a chore of keeping the yard clear of any growth. We would cut young dogwood brush into about four foot-long pieces, tie them together with binder twine or wire, and fashion them into a broom. The girls would usually do the sweeping, and the boys pulled weeds and grass. Some girls would get really creative and sweep their yards in patterns. Swirls and stripes were added as sort of a trademark. A right good fight could be generated by riding through their creations on a bike and sliding through the more artistic portions of their designs.

Anyway, while Larry and I were playing marbles, Uncle Luther was working a short distance away in a field with a mule and a plow. The hot sun, a rocky field, and a stubborn mule are enough to damage a man's mood. Add thirst to the mix, and oh boy! Well, Uncle Luther yelled out to Aunt Duddy, "Bring me some water!"

"What?" asked Aunt Duddy.

"Bring me some d**n water, you leather-headed b***h!"

"It would take a leather-headed b***h to marry a son of a b***h like you!" yelled Aunt Duddy.

At this point I felt that I was far enough from both of them to survive the bolt of lightning that was surely coming. Aunt Duddy went to the spring, filled a quart canning jar with cool water, and took it to the field for Uncle Luther. Uncle Luther drank the water with gusto. My little heart sank as he reached for Aunt Duddy. He grabbed her by the neck, pulled her forward, and started to kiss her. They smooched for awhile and parted with a "See you at suppertime, sweetheart." I stayed overnight with Larry and heard groans coming from their bedroom. As I grew older and learned about the birds and the bees, I came to believe that cussing and fighting were, for Uncle Luther and Aunt Duddy, foreplay.

Uncle Luther raised a little tobacco and also worked at Dan River Mills. With income from these two sources, he could afford a used car. Not many people coming off the Great Depression had a car. When Uncle Luther went somewhere in his old Plymouth, I was invited along for the ride. Gasoline was rationed, and so were car trips. Uncle Luther generally traveled the

exact same route every week and bought his ration of fuel at the same time and place every week. If an additional trip was taken, he occasionally ran out of gasoline. This occurred three times while I was riding with him. He ran out of gas just before crossing Wolf Island Creek. Each time he drifted right up to a huge briar vine that grew from the road bank and hung over into the road. The third time we ran out of gas and drifted up to that same briar, Uncle Luther jumped out of the car using a string of cuss words that I had never heard. The words came so fast and furious that they were largely unintelligible. He jumped up and down on that briar, calling it every word he could think of until it was ground into the dirt road. For years after that episode, I was afraid of that kind of briar. In my young mind, I truly believed that briar caused us to run out of gas. If a briar could cause you to run out of gas, no telling what kind of other mischief it could do.

Aunt Duddy told us decades later that one day she went somewhere, leaving ninety-year-old Uncle Luther alone. She returned to find Uncle Luther lying face down on the ground in the backyard. He explained that he had been on a ladder cleaning gutters. When he stepped off the last rung of the ladder while coming down, he fell and couldn't get up.

Aunt Duddy asked, "What were you doing with your hands when I walked up?"

Uncle Luther replied, "I thought, since I couldn't get up, I would pull these weeds and grass out of the shrubbery." Now that is the spirit I hope I inherited.

The last time Lucille and I visited Uncle Luther in his home, he was living alone with his cat. He was ninety-four at the time. He had left the door unlocked so we could come in. He called out, "Verne, come on back." When I got in the bedroom, Uncle Luther said, "I want to show you how an old man puts his pants on." He sat on the side of the bed and dropped his pants onto his left foot. He lifted his foot in the air as he rolled onto his back and started his right leg into his pant leg. He worked with his feet until he got his pants close enough that he could reach them with his hands and finish the task.

I said, "Uncle Luther, I could have helped you."

Uncle Luther replied, "You won't be here when I have to put them on again." That was Uncle Luther. Where there is a will, there is a way.

My wife and I visited Uncle Luther and Aunt Duddy regularly until Aunt Duddy died at eighty-seven and Uncle Luther died at ninety-six. At Uncle Luther's funeral I smiled a good deal as I reflected on the many entertaining episodes that I witnessed in their lives. I looked at Uncle Luther's cold, lifeless body and thought, *It took ninety-six years, but he finally ran out of gas for the last time.*

There were so many great memories. Every time I stepped into their house I would get a coming-home feeling and always felt loved. I miss you two.

Missing Pieces

One of the most vivid memories of my childhood took place when I was six years old. I remember being sick a great deal and having a very sore throat. My parents took me to old Dr. Dillard in Draper, North Carolina. Dr. Dillard put what felt like a boat oar in my mouth and asked me to say "Aahh" as if I had room in my mouth for any sound at all to come out. He had a terrible frown on his face and whispered something to Mama and Daddy behind my back. We left Draper and rode home in total silence.

At six years old my imagination was at full throttle. In the winter my family would listen to radio programs like *The Squeaking Door*, a frightening program for a child to hear. Often Daddy would tuck me in bed, and I would immediately descend under the covers and imagine all sorts of horrible things. The doctor's visit set my imagination in motion. I eventually worked up a belief that I was going to die.

At home for the next few days, there was plenty of private talk between Mama and Daddy. I assumed they were discussing the results of my examination. In those days, parents did not discuss things with their kids. They just acted, and the kids were left to sort things out as events unfolded. So it was with my condition.

About a week after the doctor visit I was kept from school, and Daddy and Mama took me to Leakesville, North Carolina. We arrived at a large building. I thought, *This is where you take people to die.* We met with a kindly old nurse, and I was told, "Young man, we are going to remove your tonsils." My reaction was, "Thank you, Jesus; I ain't gonna die." What are tonsils? What kind of life can a kid have without tonsils? I was assured that I would not hurt; in fact, I would not feel a thing. The nurse explained to me that tonsils were not needed and that I would be perfectly fine without them. I was also promised ice cream when the operation was over.

During the whole time I was not told that the doctor was going to cut off part of my winkie.

I was put to sleep for the procedure. The nurse was right; I never felt a thing—until I awakened the next morning. I felt that my tonsils had been cut out with pruning shears and cauterized with a blowtorch! That ice cream I was promised didn't sound like anything I wanted at that time.

Not only was my throat in terrible pain, I had a horrible pain in my pee-pee.

When a nurse came in to see me, I asked her a question that would haunt me for years. She asked, "How is our little man this morning?" I asked her, "Did you ever have your tonsils took out?" She replied, "Yes, when I was a little girl." Then I asked the big question, "Did it make your goober sore?"

Well, that story got back to Mr. Walter Smart, proprietor of the country store, where everyone in the Bend traded. He felt compelled to tell that story to everyone who came into his store. He especially enjoyed telling it to a crowd in my presence. At the punch line, he would let out a guffaw, as did everyone else. I would turn red with embarrassment. I actually felt some hate toward Mr. Walter Smart.

Eventually I got over being embarrassed when the story was told, and in fact, it became funny to me.

I returned home from college once and stopped by to see an aging Mr. Walter Smart. When I went into his store, he was weighing a piece of hoop cheese for someone. He glanced up, did a double take, and said, "Hello, Verne. Did your goober ever get well?"

Whistle Britches, Nutcracker, and Pee Wee

I acquired three nicknames early on in grammar school. During the forties and fifties, kids could be brutal about a noticeable characteristic in another kid. If your ego, self-esteem, or feelings were hurt, you took it on the chin or fought it out. We didn't have bleeding-heart counselors to come around and ask, "How do you feel about what just happened?"

It was sorta like a comedian I heard lately explaining how it was growing up in the ghetto years ago. If there were a shooting during recess, the teacher would turn it into a math class. The teacher would say, "Kids, before recess we had thirty-eight kids in class. Two got shot. How many does that leave?"

All little boys where I attended school wore overalls made of blue denim, the same blue denim used to make today's blue jeans. The overall version had a bib and suspenders. You see small kids wearing fancy ones today made by a company called OshKosh. During World War II, many items were in short supply or rationed. Blue denim was in short supply when I was to enter the fourth grade. By the time my parents sold their tobacco and went shopping for my usual two pairs of overalls, there was no blue denim to be had. The only overalls available were made of white denim. There was no such thing as going to my mama and saying, "Mother, I refuse to wear white overalls to school." You took what you were given, period. To add insult to injury, my mother sewed almost all of my three sisters' clothes and an occasional shirt for me. Mama never got the hang of sewing boys' shirts. The collars always came out with rounded collar points, looking more like a girl's blouse than a boy's shirt.

I got off the school bus for my first day in the fourth grade with the name LaVerne, being the only boy wearing white denim overalls, and wearing a Little Lord Fauntleroy shirt. I had the mark on me! The first day wasn't over before everyone was calling me "Whistle Britches." Needless to say, this led to fights. Fighting made it worse; then I had to attend school the remainder of the week wearing white overalls with green grass stains.

Since I was little for my age and some boys in the fourth grade were old enough to be in the sixth grade, the fights ended badly for me.

In the forties, if you didn't make passing grades, you were held back. This continued until you turned sixteen and could legally drop out of school. We had boys who were shaving in the fifth grade. Some parents insisted that their child stay in school, however long it took, to get a good education. This resulted in boys graying, balding, and developing hearing loss in the ninth grade. By the tenth grade we could have used an Alzheimer's section. I had one thing going for me. I made straight A's, and my teachers told me constantly that I could become anything I desired. My main desire at the time was to whip Kelly Powell's ass.

After fighting a large boy in school one day, I cried and told my daddy. Daddy told me, "LaVerne, you are tough, and I am going to explain to you how to win those fights." Daddy never had parenting classes.

He took me into the backyard to practice his technique with me. I was told to bend way over, cover the top of my head with my arms, and just take the licking until my opponent tired out or quit. It is difficult to hit someone hard while hitting down at them. We trained several days. After this training, the next time I got in a fight I applied Daddy's method. I hunkered down, took the beating until my attacker got winded, and then I used the final part of the technique. I came up full force into his balls with my knee. I applied Dad's method for three fights. That's all it took for a new nickname to be given to me: "Nutcracker." The fighting over white denim overalls soon stopped.

I still think that kids have a better shot at life if they are allowed to work out some of their differences among themselves, even if it involves fighting. As I remember, I wound up being friends with all the boys I fought. Without being taught by teachers, reading it in books, or being counseled by psychiatrists, I eventually learned that diplomacy works better than fighting.

"Nutcracker" didn't last long. I was obviously small for my age. As most all little boys do, I used to go with my daddy almost everywhere he went. I once went with my daddy on a trip to the Union Street Farmers' Store in Danville, Virginia. My daddy knew people from all over. He had been a star baseball player in high school and later played semipro baseball for a Danville team. We met an old acquaintance of Daddy's in the Union Street feed store. They laughed and traded stories from their past.

Finally, the man looked at me and asked, "Perry, is that your little boy?"

Daddy patted me on the head and said, "Yes, this is my son, LaVerne."

I could have died when the man said, "Perry, you didn't hardly get your seed back, did you?"

If I had said what I was thinking, I would have said, "And Daddy, who is this fat, ugly SOB?"

As my small stature for my age was noticed more, I someway or somehow acquired the nickname "Pee Wee." Everyone, including my best friends, called me Pee Wee until I reached high school. "Pee Wee" felt good to me, especially when called this by my best friends, Jimmy Pruitt and Curtis Richmond. I think I was called Pee Wee in an affectionate way. At least I never fought over being called Pee Wee. I saw Curtis and Jimmy years later at a high school reunion. Both called me LaVerne. I felt a sad and nostalgic longing for the days when I was still Whistle Britches, Nutcracker, or Pee Wee to them.

First Bicycle

In 1947 my older sister Betty Jean and I got sparkling new Schwinn bicycles. She was thirteen, and I was ten. Her bicycle was a royal blue girls' model, and mine was a red boys' model. I don't know if it is the same today, but back then there was a big difference between a girl's bike and a boy's bike. The girl's bike was built with no top bar. Most girls of the day wore only skirts, and this allowed a girl to mount a bike without raising her leg to an undignified position. The boy's model had a top bar that required throwing your leg up high to clear the bar when mounting. We boys developed our own macho mounting style, often copying our favorite cowboy movie star of the day—Roy Rogers, Hopalong Cassidy, or Gene Autry. I personally was a Cassidy fan because he wore black and looked a tad rebellious.

My bicycle was a twenty-eight-inch model. My parents' theory was like all the parents of that era. Buy big. They will grow into it. My problem was, how do I ride a twenty-eight-inch bike with my fourteen-inch legs? There were several ways to conquer this problem. You could embarrass yourself like James did and mount by standing on a stump, a porch, or some starting point high enough to allow one to reach the pedal on the opposite side of the bike. This required that the pedal on the side opposite the mounting side be a little past top dead center. The preferred style was to push the bike forward to a sufficient speed, catch the pedal on the mounting side of the bike a little before bottom dead center, quickly stand on the pedal and ride it to near bottom with the mounting side foot, and throw your other leg over the top bar, hoping to land it accurately on the pedal rising on the other side. If you missed, as most learners did when honing this skill, you would come crashing down and land on your growing area. You could always identify the boys who were perfecting the more macho bike mounting method. They walked with a wider stance. This condition was so prevalent in the river bend where I grew up that we dubbed it BBB. We didn't know what an acronym was, but to us it was code for "Bicycle Blue Balls." The BBB Syndrome is distinguished from the GAHS, which is caused by seesawing from side to side of the top bar while riding the pedals. No one in my circle of friends could sit on the seat and pedal their bikes at the same time. So, when you were drifting down a hill, you could sit on the seat, raise your feet, and let the pedals whirl. This was precarious going down a

long hill, because in order to stop, you had to stop the whirling pedals with your feet to apply the brakes. By the way if you haven't guessed it, GAHS is an acronym that stands for "Gaulded Ass Hole Syndrome." This condition could be identified by seeing a boy walking straddle-legged while tugging at the seat of his jeans, and wearing a tortured frown.

It was our luck that we had a weeklong rain from the very day our bikes arrived. It rained for days, preventing us from riding our new bikes. One day Mama and Daddy went to Danville and left Betty Jean in charge. My sister and I had a rivalry of biblical proportions, reminiscent of Jacob and Esau or Cain and Abel. On this day we didn't fight. As soon as Mama and Daddy left, we brought our bikes inside and rode them in the house. This was a grand trip of about fifteen feet. When our parents returned, they could readily see that we had not been fighting, which was a first. Then Mama noticed the black marks on the floor. I'm sure she immediately knew what had happened, but the joy of not having to hear accusations and counteraccusations from my sister and me prevented her complaints. She just diligently went about cleaning the spots.

The rains stopped on Sunday morning just before church. Betty Jean and I played sick to no avail. Being dead and awaiting your own funeral was the only acceptable excuse in our home for not attending church.

If you know anything about south central Virginia, you know something about sticky, red, gummy clay. I met a man in Pittsburgh, Pennsylvania, at a business lunch who came from a neighborhood close to where I grew up. He said that one time he was driving through the Bend just to see what that strange little piece of earth was all about. As he rounded a curve on the narrow, hilly, muddy road, he saw a giant mud ball rolling out of a field. The giant mud ball came to rest in the road. Having no way to turn around and afraid to back up, he was forced to sit there. Suddenly, in his words, "The mud ball commenced to working, and eventually a man, a mule, and a plow came out of that giant mud ball."

I am using this little illustration to set your imagination to wondering how little kids could ride a bike in that mire. Not to worry. Do you know what a nanosecond is? I do. It is the time it takes that sticky mess to turn from mud into fine red dust in the high places. The dips keep it mucky for awhile. When you ride a bike under these conditions, you are constantly passing through dust, mud, dust, mud, and so on. When in mud, the tires pick up the mud and carry it into the dust. The dust turns the mud into a semiplaster that cakes up between the tires and the fenders. The space between each tire and fender is reduced until one day your tire will pick up a small stone, but there is not enough space for the stone to continue around. This locks the wheel, and if you are going really fast, which is the main reason for riding a bike, the wheel will suddenly lock, and over the handlebars you will go toward a hard landing. The preventive solution to wheel locking was to take the beautiful fenders off the bike. Most of the bikes in the Bend eventually had their fenders removed.

Another problem presented by the dust and mud was worn-out pedals. The pedals were made with the bearings on both ends unsealed. The ball bearings were even visible. This design allowed dirt to get inside and quickly wear the bearings out. This called for removing the pedals, leaving a hard iron stem about one-half inch in diameter on which to ride. I remind you that everyone rode with bare feet in the summertime. Getting a new pedal was often out of the question. If you weren't skilled at this riding style, you risked your bare foot slipping off and hitting the dirt really hard, removing some flesh from your toes and simultaneously landing your whole body crotch first on the top bar of the bike.

Someone in the Bend reported that the state of North Carolina had put asphalt on a road about four miles from our homes. When I first heard the word, my ears heard "ass fault," and I thought it was something like the hemorrhoids that my uncle had. After having "asphalt" explained, we boys couldn't wait to plan a trip over to ride on a hard-surfaced road. None of us had ever done that before. The tension and excitement reached a fever pitch as we approached that beautiful dust- and mud-free road. It was truly a thing of beauty. Our hearts raced as we hand rolled our bikes onto that smooth road. The first shock was to see what ninety-six degrees does to asphalt and the effects it has on bare feet. We immediately rolled our bikes forward and used our own unique mounting style to get going. My style was the roll forward, catch the mounting side pedal (correction—stem) at a little before bottom dead center, throw my bare right foot over the top bar, and catch the stem a little past top dead center on the opposite side. I then put all my weight on my right foot. When my right foot was at about five o'clock, my foot slipped off. All five of my toes hit the hot tar at the same time. This caused a loss of a little piece of meat on each toe. Simultaneously, I fell crotch first on the top crossbar. I abandoned the bike and at full-scream mode danced on my left foot on the hot tar and clasped my bleeding right foot with my right hand while holding my crotch with my left hand. I was told that I danced off the road onto cool grass in about twenty steps at about Mach 1.5, while never letting go of my crotch and right foot.

I became a legend in the Bend and points beyond, but it was an unwanted title. My dance steps that day have never been duplicated to my knowledge. Some break dancers and possibly a few rappers have come close.

I was tended by an angel who lived in a nearby farmhouse on that infamous day; I love her even now. I pedaled that same asphalt road with great success and pleasure four months later in November of that year.

Tire Ups and Downs

When you grow up without store-bought toys, you have to be creative. In my neighborhood, the status symbol was used car tires. You could tie one to a tree limb with a rope and make a swing that could repeatedly take you up and down whether you were standing up or sitting down; you could roll them around and pretend to be driving a Packard, a Chevrolet, or a Ford. If you had a kid little enough and dumb enough, you could put him in the tire by placing the top of his head in the top of the tire and his feet inside the bottom and roll him down a hill. Also there were people so poor that they lived in old slave cabins. These cabins had a back door in line with a middle door and a front door. Very often they left these doors open in the summer and had no screen doors. With the right timing and a little incline toward the house, you could roll the tire clean through the house. This was one of my personal favorites until one day one of our tires didn't come out the other side. For awhile I suffered the humiliation of being tireless. Your status rose with the number of tires you had but could be offset by having the largest tire. If you had one regular tire and, say, a big truck tire, you were really somebody.

One of our adult neighbors was Jimmy Hunt. We kids were afraid of Mister Jimmy; he had beady eyes and shouted at us. There was a rumor that he ate kids; that's what we all believed. It didn't matter that no kids ever disappeared from our neighborhood; we believed it. Jimmy had a little blond-headed girl brat who was easily talked into things. She was mean and would run to her dad and bring his meanness down on us. It became our belief that if we couldn't get even with Jimmy, we could get his little girl—so we hatched up a disgusting plan. It was polkberry season. (We used to make a deep purple ink from the polkberries. We would find a rooster feather and fashion it into a quill for writing and drawing. Polkberry vines were great; you could eat the tender leaves as a green vegetable.) Jimmy Hunt raised goats. Goat turds were perfectly round and fairly smooth. My oldest sister and I experimented with adding sugar to the polkberry juice and dyeing goat turds with it. They were beautiful. We showed the dyed turds to Jimmy's little brat kid and told her they were candy. She just had to have some. Our plan was to watch her put them in her mouth, bite down, and then puke. She didn't puke; she wanted more. We ran so fast and stayed inside, pretending to be sick for a few days. Every time

someone came by, we thought they were bringing news of little Ann Hunt's death. She grew up to be a beautiful and sweet woman. I always wondered what role eating goat turds had to do with her development.

I digressed from the tire story. What I was getting around to was that Jimmy Hunt had a tractor. Eventually, he had to replace a tire. He must have seen me admiring that old tire, and one day he said to me, "Boy, do you want that old tractor tire?" Surely the gods were smiling on me that day. I got the biggest tire in the neighborhood and lost my fear of Mister Jimmy all in one day. I got Clarence and Theodore, my two black buddies, to help me bring the tire home. We took a long way home so as to expose my wealth to everyone. We washed that tire 'til it was clean and black. I spent an abundance of time wondering just what a boy could do with a tire like that. It was far too big to swing in. It was oversize for rolling a small kid in. Then it hit me: Helen Overby. Helen was a little slow but had a great disposition and was gung-ho to try anything just to get to play with us. That's it; I will get Clarence and Theodore to help me get the tire up the highest hill we could find, and then roll Helen down the hill inside my huge, shiny, black tractor tire.

Our plan came together. We assembled on top of the hill. Helen had a unique way of grunting loudly when excited. She was grunting louder than I had ever heard her. Now, we had learned to read our regular rolling hills like a professional golfer reads golf greens before putting. The chosen hill was new territory. It was steeper and longer than any other hill in our repertoire. We put Helen inside the tire and gave it our best shot of reading the lay of the land and aiming that tire. We launched the tire, and down the hill went Helen. For a few seconds all went well. We had never experienced such a thrill in our young lives. Then, as they say, all hell broke loose. The tire picked up speed going faster and faster. The centrifugal force slung Helen's arms out, making it seem as if she were about to fly. Suddenly, the tire veered slightly from the route and struck a low-cut stump dead-on center. This caused the tire to jump extremely high (we guessed fifty feet) and caused Helen to fly through the air inside the tire. When the tire touched down again, it went straight as an arrow—that is, straight toward the creek. Fear gripped us so that we couldn't speak. However, we did burst into loud crying, running as fast as we could down the long, steep hill to the creek. We expected to find Helen dead. I had already started contemplating life in prison or worse. By the time we reached the creek, which seemed like an eternity, we found a soaked Helen crawling out of a deep spot, giggling and hollering, "Let's do it again! Let's do it again!" If that tire had landed four feet farther either to the left or to the right, "So long, Helen." We retired that tractor tire for awhile. We wouldn't even walk close to it for a long time.

The Great Scarf Episode

I attended grammar school at Happy Home Elementary School. Don't confuse the name with the funny farm, although at times it sure looked like a funny farm. Happy Home was a North Carolina school. We did not have a school in the Bend, so we were allowed to attend the nearest North Carolina school by a special arrangement between North Carolina and Virginia. We Bend kids were an oddity and an aggravation to Happy Home. Special records had to be kept on us. Before these arrangements were made, Bend kids were taught in a one-room school built by the local farmers. The school was built on land owned by my maternal great-grandparents. The teachers were local parents and had not been trained to be schoolteachers. After the state of Virginia made arrangements for Bend kids to attend Happy Home Elementary School, the old schoolhouse was remodeled into a home for my maternal grandmother, Shotgun Essie, and my grandfather, Charlie. My mother grew up in the house, and eventually it became the house in which I grew up.

In the fall of my seventh-grade year, our school bought our first professionally built playground equipment. The principal put me on a team to assemble the various pieces: seesaws, swings, merry-go-rounds, jumping boards, and my delight of delights, the monkey bars. Bill Cosby tells of a kid who asked his dad, "Daddy, please take me to the park and put me on that thing that goes round and round 'til I puke." Well, there was a lot of puking the first few weeks of using that merry-go-round. Some kids got so good at the jumping boards that, if matched properly weight wise, they could go ten feet in the air. Most of us kids had never used store-bought playground equipment before. I think that most of that equipment is now outlawed on the majority of school playgrounds because "someone might get hurt" or "somebody might sue us if his child gets hurt."

For the next few weeks after the new equipment was installed, total chaos broke out at every recess. Kids came running wildly out of every classroom in an attempt to be first in line for the various pieces. There was pushing and shoving, and fights broke out. Some of the affluent kids traded their ice-cream money for someone's first-in-line spot. It got to the point that playing

on the equipment became less important than winning the enviable position of being first or next. Eventually, a teacher had to be appointed to referee at every recess.

Near the time we finished installing the playground equipment, Mrs. Caudle, the third-grade teacher, accused me of stealing little Sara Gauldin's scarf. Sara lived in the Bend about a mile from me. We rode the school bus together. The accusation stood, and punishment was pending; either the scarf showed up, or I needed to return it. The sting of having been falsely accused of stealing and my anger toward the third-grade teacher stayed fresh on my mind for days.

One day I was swinging on the new swings. Instead of swinging in the normal way, I was straddling the seat swinging back and forth in the wrong direction. Mrs. Caudle approached me and haughtily said, "Stop swinging biased [diagonally] right this minute."

With my anger toward her still heavy on my mind, I arrogantly replied, "I helped put this equipment up, and I will swing any durn way I want to!"

She went straight to the principal and reported me. Mr. Walters, the principal, was strict and tough on anything deemed bad behavior. Back talking to a teacher and using foul language ("durn") was, in his opinion, really bad behavior. I found out later that Mrs. Caudle had not told Mr. Walters that Sara's scarf had been found. He still had me under orders to return the scarf, and my punishment was still pending. Mr. Walters appeared at the swings. Taking me by the arm, he practically dragged me to his office. I tried to discuss the great scarf episode, but he would hear none of it.

He took out his paddle that, at the moment, looked to be eight feet long with nails sticking out of it. He said, "LaVerne, you are a really good student, and this is going to hurt me more than it is going to hurt you."

By this time, I could care less about what he or that monster teacher thought, so I sarcastically replied, "I'll trade places with you then."

My "smart" comment eliminated all his compassion, and I got my due for sure. Well, a kid cannot let a thing like that just lie there. Some form of revenge was in order. After all, I was a Bend kid; Bend kids settle scores.

Mrs. Caudle had just gotten a new black Plymouth automobile. It was a warm fall day; we had rain the night before, and she parked that shiny new car right by a mud puddle. Do you see it coming? At the first recess I went into the woods, took my Barlow knife out, and cut myself a very leafy branch. I found a big stick on the ground. I took the stick and stirred the mud puddle to a consistency slightly thinner than pancake batter. I then dipped the branch into the batter until it was well coated and commenced to splatter that new Plymouth, leaving it looking like a solid mud car. Unbeknownst to me, my nemesis saw the last few splashes of mud being applied to her formerly shiny black new Plymouth. Boy, did this act stir up a hornet's nest. The principal didn't have a clue as to what to do about me. What I was expecting was a severe beating, which I had already decided would be well worth it. What I got was worse.

Mr. Walters looked at me with total disdain. "Young man, do your parents know how bad you can be?" he asked.

"Yes, sir," was my muffled reply.

"Well, we will see about that. I am going to take you home, and you may not be allowed to return to this school. You may wind up in reformatory school, and all this is going on your permanent record."

Even before these events occurred, my permanent record must have already broken all previous records. I blurted out, "I live with my grandmother, so take me there." My thought here was that Shotgun Essie would deal with him really well, but it wasn't to be. Somehow he knew better. As we drove on the dirt road to my house, I prayed to have a stroke. I had heard that Mrs. Hyler died from a stroke, and it seemed like a way out for me. When we turned off the dusty dirt road to my house, his car was covered with so much dust that it looked about as bad as Mrs. Caudle's mud-coated car. Dread of dreads and fear of fears, my dad was driving up on the tractor as we stopped in our yard.

Fortunately, my dad was very wise and would always hear things out thoroughly and keep an open mind. Mr. Walters detailed the whole story. He told Daddy about the scarf stealing, the swinging improperly, and the talking back to Mrs. Caudle. He told of the whipping I got and the latest car-mudding act. I had my fingers crossed and prayed to myself, *Please, God, don't let him tell about the "durn" word.* He ended with, "And that scarf has not been returned either."

My dad listened quietly, listened to it all. He then very calmly asked, "You don't know that the scarf was found? LaVerne told me about being accused of stealing that scarf. I took him to the Gauldins' home to investigate the matter. When we got there and explained our reason for coming, Sara's grandfather said that he knew that LaVerne had been accused of stealing the scarf. He also said that he found the scarf that very day where his granddaughter had dropped it on the way to meet the school bus. Furthermore, he took his granddaughter to school and explained everything to Mrs. Caudle so LaVerne would be cleared." Further talk revealed that my bad behavior occurred well after Mrs. Caudle knew these things, but had never told Mr. Walters.

Mr. Walters was quiet for a moment, then shook my dad's dirty hand and said, "I think I understand things a little better now."

Mr. Walters drove me back to school without saying a word. He took me to my classroom. When we arrived, he very quietly said, "All will be forgotten if you will help me wash Mrs. Caudle's car this afternoon. Your father knows that I will bring you home."

When I got home, my father said, "Next time you have any kind of problem, talk to me about it before you dig a hole too deep to get out of by yourself." I suppose my dad introduced me to the principle, "When you find yourself in a hole almost too deep to get out of, stop digging."

I still had many more problems after these incidents, but I was never afraid to talk to my daddy about anything again. I only hope that I used a little of my father's wisdom in raising my own kids.

School Lunches

Almost all rural, southern, farm kids of my generation shared many of the same experiences growing up. I have a friend I call my walking buddy. We grew up 150 miles apart, a world away from each other back then, but akin in spirit and experiences. For about thirteen years, until he developed circulatory problems and had to quit, he, I, and another old friend walked four miles per day, four days a week, for our health. We often reminisced and shared stories about our childhoods on tobacco farms. One day the subject of school lunches came up. Again our experiences were the same. We did not have cafeterias in our schools, so lunch was brought from home. The kids from families whose parents were in "public work," as it was called back then, usually brought their lunches in fancy lunch pails. Those lunch boxes were often painted with pictures of Roy Rogers, Dick Tracy, Alley Oop, or some other comic-book character. We farm kids were issued brown paper sacks on Monday that, after use, were to be folded neatly and tucked in the back pockets of our bib overalls. These same bags were used for the entire week.

The kids with lunch pails had sandwiches made with pretty sliced white bread filled with exotic foods like bologna, mayonnaise, peanut butter, and cold cuts made from things that we poor kids could only imagine. We farm kids were stuck with meager lunches made with homemade biscuits containing either leftovers from dinner the night before or breakfast that morning. They were filled with dinner things such as steak from a cow that we slaughtered, tenderloin from a hog we had killed, or fried chicken from our yard flock. Biscuits filled with breakfast leftovers would contain country ham, pork sausage, or maybe fried rabbit that Daddy had killed early that morning. I remember well seeing the farm kids trying to hide their humble meals as they ate them. We had to take homemade pies while the fancy lunch pails contained store-bought Moon Pies and other delicacies.

Most of our food was raised right in front of our eyes and under our hoes. We had, as they say, up-close and personal relationships with what we ate. We used whatever technology was available at the time to can, dry, salt down, smoke, and preserve everything grown on the land. A well-thought-out plan would allow a farm family to have enough food to last from season to season and from crop to crop.

During the Great Depression of 1929 and the following lean years, farm families would often share with relatives and people in need. These acts of sharing would sometimes cause families to run short of certain foods, and they would have to improvise with school lunches. My walking buddy told me that his family had needed to share their meat with kin who had fallen on hard times, and so his family ran out of meat before the school year ended. They were stuck with whatever was available. He said that he took collard biscuits to school day after day until he was sick and tired of collard biscuits. He remembered one morning when a kid came to school and placed a really heavy-looking lunch bag on the cloakroom shelf. When the lunch bell rang, my friend grabbed the heavy-looking lunch, ran deep into the woods, hid behind a big oak tree, and settled down to what he expected to be a feast. When he opened the bag, he suffered a tremendous disappointment; he found ten hickory nuts and a hammer.

Note to the reader: You can now get a poor, rural, southern farm school kid's, old-fashioned lunch at Hardee's, Biscuitville, or McDonald's.

Claustrophobia

I like to lie in bed at night and let my mind wander. I imagine that my eyes are rolled back and looking into my brain's files. I read once that all that we have ever read, seen, heard, or in any way experienced is stored and filed somewhere in our brains. Strange how many memories, long forgotten, may surface if you free your mind of every thought and let it look around. I was on a tour of my memory one night recently. Just as I was falling asleep, I suddenly found myself struggling to get through a wall vent, the kind you see in a brick wall that allows for ventilation under a building. I awakened abruptly, sweating profusely, and hyperventilating. For years I have suffered from claustrophobia, not simply feeling uncomfortable in close places, but experiencing debilitating and paralyzing feelings.

I used to have to fly a great deal in my work. I conquered the problem on large airliners, but there was one commuter plane I had to fly from Boston, Massachusetts, to Bangor, Maine. I believe it was a Gulfstream. The plane had one row of seats down each side. Even as short as I am, I had to stoop to walk down the aisle. The first time I faced having to fly on that plane, I panicked when I entered the plane door. I said to no one in particular, "I can't do it."

A man behind me asked, "Do you have claustrophobia?"

I replied that I did.

He said, "Run to the bar and get a shot of whiskey. That's what I do."

I had time to run back, get cleared by the gate attendant, and rush to a nearby bar. I slugged down a shot of whiskey and returned to the plane just as the door was about to close. My seat happened to be across the aisle from the man who gave me that advice. On the one-hour trip to Bangor, I did not feel panic. That was great advice and came in handy. A few years later we sold our engineering construction company to a company in Pittsburg, Kansas. I was required to travel there every two weeks for a year. I had to fly that awful little plane from St. Louis, Missouri, to Joplin, Missouri, every trip. I never flew again without two mini-bottles of whiskey in my briefcase, one for going and one for the return trip. It makes sense, you know. A little whiskey makes some people bulletproof and gives them enough courage to take on everyone in the bar.

After being awakened by the nightmare of struggling to get through the ventilator, I suddenly recalled the incident that may have caused my phobia. In the seventh grade, Jimmy Pruitt, Curtis Richmond, and I were best friends—or at least bound by a treaty. We were pretty smart and passed our grades each year. By the sixth grade we were starting to catch up to boys who had failed the first, second, and third grades. By this time we were being challenged by boys three and four years our senior. Fighting in Happy Home Elementary School was not only allowed but was tacitly approved as a way for boys to learn to resolve conflicts; girls didn't fight at our school. Jimmy, Curtis, and I teamed up to defend one another. By the fifth grade we had left many boys, who still had shaving cream in their noses from learning to shave, lying on the ground crying. As long as our alliance held, we had a period of détente with the slow learners. With any slight weakening of our treaty, we suffered the consequences individually. By the time those boys reached sixteen, they had usually dropped out of school. At the inception of the alliance, our plan always included choosing the three middle seats in the back of the classroom. This strategy worked well for the first two weeks of the school year. Our behavior resulted in our being relocated to the front row in the three seats closest to the teacher. In subsequent years we would rush into class first and stake claim to the three back-row seats farthest from the teacher.

Our reputation preceded us. The teacher would walk into the room never looking up and say, "LaVerne, Curtis, and Jimmy—I have seats reserved for you up front." The seventh-grade teacher, Mrs. Sledge, even had our names on our desks when we came to class the first day.

Now, Mrs. Sledge was a large, unmarried woman. Unfortunately, she had terrible body odor. Since my desk was the first one in the front right corner next to her desk, I got a full dose of her smell. To add further injury to my sensibilities, she would often sit on the edge of my desk while teaching. She carried a yardstick that she wielded like a Samurai sword. I noticed that she put out a particularly offensive odor when she wore a deep purple dress made from a crepe-type material. One day she was sitting on the edge of my desk with a book in one hand and her trusty ol' yardstick in the other hand. She had on that purple dress. The combination of the hot day and the purple dress caused especially efficient radiation of her BO. Since her sitting position prevented her from observing me directly, I turned to the class squeezing my nose and making my worst frown. The class erupted in laughter. Mrs. Sledge gave me a strong whack with her yardstick across my back that surely left bruises on both of my fat-free shoulder blades. The class laughed even harder.

When the lunch bell rang, I waited for everyone to leave the room, and then I discussed a plan with Jimmy and Curtis. My plan: There was about a two-inch hole in the floor, right by Mrs. Sledge's desk, left by workmen relocating a radiator. There was a high crawl space under our classroom. Jimmy and Curtis would keep watch while I sneaked back into the classroom to drop the yardstick through the hole. That would be the last time she would strike anyone with that stick. The plan worked. As often happens in war, I was not prepared for the aftermath. I had no exit strategy.

When the lunch hour ended, I was the first one seated. This alone probably raised Mrs. Sledge's suspicions. Mrs. Sledge walked to her desk and, without looking down, reached for her yardstick. No stick. With a look of *I can't believe it's not there*, she slid her hand about as if she hoped it would show up. Still no yardstick. She went into a rage, ending with, "I think I know who is responsible for this. If my yardstick does not show up, not only will this be entered in that student's permanent record, but reform school will certainly be considered."

I was not allowed to say "shitless," so I was scared "dookiless." By then I had accumulated quite a thick permanent record, but a threat of reform school was my ultimate fear. I had been told how kids in reform school had their fingernails pulled out, among other tortures. All I could think of was, *How can I get that yardstick back on her desk without being caught?*

When the bell rang for recess, I rushed outside to huddle with my allies, Jimmy and Curtis.

Jimmy said, "You could crawl under the school building and push the yardstick back up through the hole, and we'll grab it. Curtis and I will stand watch in the room until you push the stick up."

We rushed around the school building in search of an entry underneath the building. We finally found a vent hole with the metal grid missing. The vent was about two hundred feet from our classroom. I barely wiggled through the small vent hole. Using my best homing instincts, I finally got directly underneath our classroom and found the yardstick.

I tapped on the floor and heard Jimmy say, "The coast is clear."

Up through the floor went the yardstick. I heard my allies drop the stick and walk out of the room. What sweet success. No reform school for me!

By now, my skinny little body was sweating. I crawled as fast as possible back to my entry point. I started to wiggle back through. Suddenly, I got stuck. Evidently crawling for that distance and sweating had caused me to swell just enough that I no longer could fit easily through that vent hole. I thought I was going to die there. I went limp with fear. I tried again and felt my blue jeans slip on my hips. I moved some more and felt my body coming out of my jeans. I got free with only my underwear on. I reached in, retrieved my blue jeans, pulled them on, and rushed to my seat just before the bell rang. I did not see the yardstick on Mrs. Sledge's desk. By now I was puking sick. Mrs. Sledge walked in and suddenly looked down at the floor. She reached down nonchalantly as if to think, *Oh, it has probably been there all along.* Jimmy and Curtis had cleverly put it there just to create an impression that the yardstick had simply fallen from the desk. I was a model student for a couple of weeks.

At long last, I had stumbled onto the incident that may have caused my fear of being in small, confining places. Just knowing this has been a big help in conquering my claustrophobia. Now I just need to work on that snake thing.

The Disappearing Pocketbooks

One of the most beloved games among my bend-of-the-river friends was "The Disappearing Pocketbooks." We played that game until we ran through every sucker in our area.

To play this intriguing and stimulating game, you only need a ladies pocketbook (preferably a large one), about a hundred feet of strong twine, a moonlit night, and a dirt road that has slow-moving automobile traffic. The moonlit-night idea came from an episode where several of us ran head-on into trees during the escape phase on one really dark night. The pocketbook with the twine attached is laid on the edge of the road. A spot is chosen on the outside curve of the road so that an approaching car's lights would shine directly on the pocketbook. The road bank must be fairly level and have a thick brush border. The string is covered with dirt to camouflage it. A narrow path is cleared in the brush along the road border, and the twine is carried through the narrow path to where we lay in wait for an automobile to approach. When the driver happened to glimpse the pocketbook lying on the side of the road, he would always stop unless he had already been a victim of the ruse. One of the passengers would jump out of the car and reach for the pocketbook. The person holding the string would run with it, and we would scatter. The embarrassed person would look in all directions (a typical reaction), either in an attempt to see who pulled the prank or to see if anyone saw him being made to look like a fool.

One would think that we would run out of victims—not so. We wouldn't run out until everyone using that road had been hoodwinked. I suppose that no one victimized in that way would go to Mr. Walter Smart's store and tell how he had been made to look like a fool, so word never got around.

This neat little trick was used for awhile but eventually got boring. Typical of our normal modus operandi, we started to improvise on the standard procedure. Sonny loved snakes, so it seemed natural to put a snake in the pocketbook minus the string attached and let the poor victim win for once.

The first automobile that approached was occupied by the driver only. He got out, picked the pocketbook up, got back in his car, and drove off. What a failure. No chance to see the fright on his face. We still believed in ourselves. We had used the same pocketbook hitherto.

Now we had to replace that fine old, tough leather bag, but this was not easy. It was at the end of the Great Depression, and not many women had a purse. Shotgun Essie, my grandmother, was the only person we could count on to aid and abet us in our foolishness. She enjoyed hearing every detail of our ventures, and as far as we know she never told on us. We got our new tool from her with a promise by us to visit and share our experience.

Our next night out was a success. We placed the pocketbook in the road with a small, harmless garden snake in it. The first car stopped, a passenger got out, picked up the pocketbook, and got back in the car. So it was another failed attempt to frighten the hell out of someone. Suddenly the car slid to a stop. Everyone in the car, five of them, jumped out screaming and cursing. Suddenly, one of the men came full speed in our direction. My heart had never raced so fast in my life. Fortunately, we eluded our pursuer and gathered at our preplanned meeting place.

Sonny searched all week but could not find a snake for our next planned night out. We were disappointed, but ol' Hermon "the Gross" came up with a solution.

Hermon, a young man of limited vocabulary, said, "Let's put a turd in it."

At first, no one cared for this gross idea. After a few days of hard farmwork and extreme boredom, we reconsidered. My justification was in the interest of scientific research. Just how would a person faced with the expectation of a found treasure react upon putting his hand into that sort of stuff? Little by little we all caved in to Hermon's plan. Hermon was the only one with the constitution to put the plan in place. He was not much of a leader, so he relished the idea of leading such a venture. James puked during the setup.

On a warm, moonlit night in summer, the historic event took place. We set everything up and waited. We had enough light from the moon to see a black Packard approach. We knew it was the minister at Blue Stone Baptist Church and his family. We loved that man. He was kind to children, and most of us played with his kids. We couldn't let what was about to happen, happen to this man.

Just as the minister got out of the car and picked up the pocketbook, Sonny jumped into the road and said, "Shotgun Essie lost this pocketbook. I will take it to her." Rev. Hairston scratched his head, got back into his car, and drove off. Hermon, of course, had cleanup detail.

It took some time, but we talked ourselves out of abandoning our new plan. On the next pocketbook-with-turd adventure, everything was spot-on. Not long after the setup, a car approached. It was not someone we knew, so we felt no obligation to abort the mission. The car stopped; someone got out, picked up the pocketbook, and got back in the car. The car slowly moved away. We were sorely disappointed. Suddenly, the car slid to a stop. Everyone in the car jumped out. One of them was shaking his hand furiously. I had never heard such creative cursing, not even from my Uncle Crawford's fox-hunting friends. James puked as we observed several of the victims have a puke fest. They were strangers to us as well as we could tell. They looked around and saw us in the moonlight and tore out after us. We got away, but it was a close call.

This time someone told. The word got around that the hoodlums would be found, and they would reap their just reward. My dad told me what he had heard at Mr. Walter Smart's store. He looked at me sternly and said, "LaVerne, I suppose you didn't have anything to do with that, did you?" He probably saw the answer on my face, but he turned and walked away before I could answer. It took a long time for the furor over that incident to die down. I decided that I would wait maybe about thirty years before participating in "The Disappearing Pocketbooks" again.

My Permanent Record

Throughout my grammar school years I heard, "Young man, this is going in your permanent record," many, many times. It was always because of something that was in some way considered misbehavior. I made nearly perfect scores in grammar school. The teacher would drop a test paper on my desk with a big red "100%" on it and, with a sarcastic tone say, "I don't know how you do it." The teacher never said, "LaVerne, this is so good it is going in your permanent record." With these experiences, why wouldn't a kid suspect that permanent records are only for noting misbehaviors?

I used to worry, *What if my mama and daddy were to see my permanent record?* or, horror of horrors, *What if Granny Pruitt ever sees it?* I imagined that when you were passed on to a higher grade, the teachers discussed former pupils.

I could just imagine my fourth-grade teacher saying to Mrs. Stevens, my fifth-grade teacher, "LaVerne will do well as long as you threaten him with his permanent record." I lived in fear of my permanent record being exposed, such as in the newspaper. I could imagine my picture with the caption saying, "Happy Home student in *Guinness Book of World Records* for accumulating the largest permanent record of misbehaviors in history at only ten years old." There would be an asterisk with a footnote saying, "Second place for most times threatened with reform school."

My dad asked me once—no, he told me—"Go with me to Wentworth to the records office, LaVerne."

I shivered in fear; I will never forget that day. It was a Friday, the first day after school was out in the spring. I had just received my last-of-the-school-year permanent record warnings for snapping Nancy Evans's bra strap. "Young man, this is going into your permanent record," said Mrs. Sledge. Nancy was the first to wear a bra in our class. After years of making and shooting sling shooters, it came sort of natural for me to snap it.

Well, as we drove off, I started to tremble in fear. *He's going to look at my permanent record*, I thought.

I was so quiet for the forty-five-minute trip to Wentworth, North Carolina, that Daddy asked me several times, "LaVerne, are you all right?"

"Yes, Daddy, I'm just tired from a long school year." I was thinking all along, *Daddy is testing me. He wants me to confess, come clean, be contrite, or something.*

We got to the courthouse, parked, and started in. I was thinking, *I always carry a pocket knife; maybe I should end it all right now.*

As we entered the building, Daddy asked the first person we met, "Where do you keep the records?"

"In the vault down those stairs," replied the woman.

It took what seemed like forever to get down those stairs. As we entered the room, I saw shelves and shelves of huge binders. By then, I was on the verge of hyperventilating. Daddy

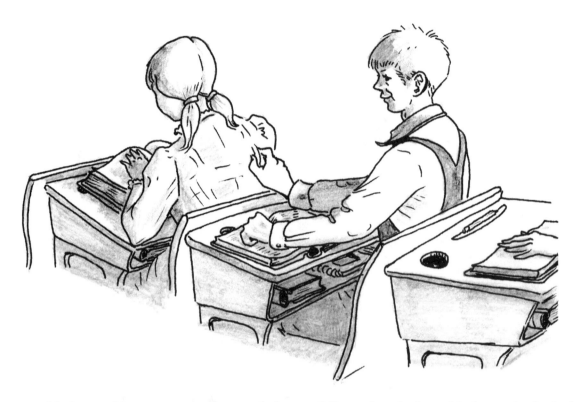

mumbled something to an attendant, and she carefully retrieved a large binder as she looked bitchily toward me. I knew the jig was up for me. I walked casually along the rows of binders, much as one would whistle through a graveyard. Not knowing how they filed permanent records, I looked for binders lettered "T" for Thornton and "L" for LaVerne. There appeared to be two volumes for each letter. I didn't see which volume was pulled for Daddy. I only knew that he was viewing the one he had with a serious look.

Daddy finished his review of the record, and we left. I was preparing for the worst. I sat so quietly that Daddy asked, "LaVerne, are you sure that you are okay?"

"Yes, Daddy."

"You look pale to me," he exclaimed. I assumed that he wanted to review his discovery with Mama before he meted out my punishment. We rode quietly for awhile, and finally Daddy cleared his throat.

Here it comes, I thought.

"You know what, LaVerne? According to the record I looked at, that land I leased has more tobacco allotment than I thought. It is going to be a good deal." A sweet relief swept over me. I babbled the rest of the way home.

When we got home, Daddy told Mama, "LaVerne looked sick on the way to Wentworth, but he seems to be much better now."

That experience didn't completely dispel my fears that my permanent record would one day pop up and bite me. I once had a dream that I was offered a great opportunity in Des Moines, Iowa. I had the right credentials, right degree, and right experiences. I was a perfect match for a top position in that huge corporation. There was only one thing left—an interview with the company president. I flew to Des Moines for the interview. As I pulled into the parking lot early to be sure of being on time for the interview, I saw an eighteen-wheeler parked there that had a sign painted on the side that said, "LaVerne Thornton's Permanent Record." I turned to leave and suddenly awakened in a cold sweat.

After I attained enough success in business to feel comfortable that I had outlived any detrimental effect my permanent record may have had on my career, I still wondered about what might be in it. When I was in my early forties, I had my secretary call the Rockingham County Schools superintendent's office to request a copy of my permanent record. After much discussion with several employees of the school system, my secretary said they confessed to having no knowledge whatsoever of having permanent records on everyone. Furthermore, they stated that if anything like my permanent record ever existed, it would be personal information that was accumulated when I was a youth, and it could never be released to anyone.

Even with this knowledge, I still occasionally, if I do something devilish or naughty, hear Mrs. Sledge say, "Young man, this is going in your permanent record."

Turning Twelve

The day I turned twelve years old, February 17, 1949, my daddy asked me to go for a walk with him. I had received several promises that certain things I had done wrong in school that week would certainly find its way into my permanent record. Daddy had such a serious expression on his face that I felt sure he was going to confront me about something I had done. We walked to the river and sat on a rock by a spot where the Dan River flowed over a rocky section, forming rapids. This place, I had learned, was my daddy's place for inspiration. A strange calmness came over me as we sat for a few moments in silence.

Daddy looked out over the rapids and said, "It would be hard to find a place better than this." He then turned toward me and said, "The book of Luke in the *Bible* contains an account of Jesus's childhood, an incident in the Temple in Jerusalem. The story tells of how Joseph and Mary took twelve-year-old Jesus to Jerusalem for the Passover festival. While there, he disappeared for three days. They found him in the Temple, where he was discussing matters of religion with the teachers of the Law. They were amazed at his understanding and his answers." Dad then said something to me that would alter my life forever and affect the way I think and feel about life's matters, especially money. "LaVerne, you are wise beyond your years, and just as Jesus became a man at twelve years old, from now on I will consider you to be a man." Dad continued, "I am going to count off rows of tobacco this crop year to be your personal crop. The crop from these rows will be kept separate all the way through to selling time. The money from the sale will be all yours. With that money you will pay for everything you need for clothes, school expenses, and spending money. You can do anything you want to with the money. I have figured that there will be enough to pay for your needs if you budget carefully. If you run out of money before the next crop is sold, I will loan you enough to see you through. You must remember that if you borrow money from me, you must pay it back; so you will start the next year short." After a brief silence he asked, "Do you have any questions?"

"No, Daddy," I replied.

"Well, what do you think, little man?"

I could only mumble a feeble, "Thank you, Daddy."

At twelve years old I could do almost the same work as any man. I could harness the mules and break land for a garden or any other crop. I could plant any crop at the right time and the right way. I could cut and prepare firewood, tend farm animals, milk cows, and churn butter. My mother insisted that I do any work the girls did, so I could wash, iron, cook, and do a limited amount of sewing. Flat tires were a big problem back then, so I could dismount a tire, patch the tube, and remount the wheel and tire as well as any man. My dad would make me so proud when he would say to other men at Mr. Walter Smart's store, "I had rather have LaVerne work with me than any other man I know." I would tackle anything, but this responsibility for my own money nearly scared the life from me. I knew Daddy's word was solid and sure. I also knew that he would not let me fail. My attitude was that I have to and I will make it work.

Everything seemed different at that moment. At the time, I had never heard the word "surreal." Looking back, though, it is a perfect word for how the world seemed to me at that time. I started to act and think differently. Even my teachers noticed a change in me. I received fewer threats of placing my misbehaviors into my permanent record. My voice had started to change pitch in the middle of sentences, so that added to my new manly persona.

Throughout the summer I thought and planned how to spend the money that I would get when we sold tobacco. As it would in any twelve-year-old boy's mind, a new bicycle, a hunting rifle, fishing items, and other things that I might buy floated through my thoughts. Gradually thoughts of all the fun things I could buy faded away and were replaced by the fear that I might run out of money. My formative years were right on the heels of the Great Depression and during World War II; fear was a constant human condition in our world. We had a severe drought during my first crop year, which meant that there was a real chance for a meager tobacco crop and less income. By midsummer I started to think of ways to earn money to supplement my needs.

We had two publications coming into our home, *the Progressive Farmer* and the *Danville Register* newspaper. I read every word in the *Progressive Farmer*, even the advertisements. Two ads caught my attention. One small ad simply said, "Make money selling Zanol Home Products. Send for details." I responded to the ad, and within a few days I received a reply along with a catalog and a sales manual. They offered me a job selling Zanol products. I was to take the catalog around, solicit orders, and send the orders in along with their part of the money. When the products came back to me, I would deliver them and collect my money. It was hard work pedaling around the Bend selling and delivering those home products, but in my life it was easy money and it started to add up.

Another ad in *the Progressive Farmer* was looking for people to operate (run) punchboards. If you do not know what punchboards are, the following information found on the Internet at www.punchboard.com/ explains them:

WHAT IS A PUNCH BOARD?

The term "punchboard" (or in some cases "punch board," "push board," "punch-card," or "push card") refers to a gambling device popular in the United States from roughly 1900 until 1970.

Punchboards were particularly popular during the 1930s, 1940s, and 1950s. Although they are illegal to operate in many states, you can still find punchboards being played today in some areas of the country, particularly as fund-raisers for clubs and organizations. Punchboards are also beginning to gain popularity in countries outside the United States.

A punchboard generally consists of a square piece of wood or cardboard in which hundreds or thousands of holes have been drilled and filled with slips of rolled or folded paper. Each slip of paper has a number or combination of symbols printed on it. The holes are covered with a foil or paper seal, which protects the corresponding slips. Punchboards usually have a chart listing the combinations of numbers or symbols that are considered winners, along with the prizes or cash amounts that will be awarded to the winners.

Typical board construction is of laminated cardboard built up to a thickness of ⅝ to 1 inch with a series of holes drilled through the board to accommodate the folded-up set of paper slips. Some punchboards use a separate payout card with jackpot seals or a separate payout board.

Here's how the game works: A player pays the punchboard's operator a set amount of money (usually a nickel, dime, or quarter) for a chance to use a metal stylus (or "punch") to break the seal on the hole of his choice and "punch" one of the slips of paper out of the board. If the number or symbols found on the slip of paper matches one of the predetermined winning combinations, the player is awarded the corresponding prize.

I responded to the punchboard ad, and I was soon the go-to guy for buying a chance to win a prize on the punchboard. I ran boards that had nickel, dime, and up to a quarter per punch. I finished the first board, took my commission, and sent the company's part in. When I received the prizes to be distributed to the winners, I realized that the value of the prizes was worth about one-fourth the value of the money I sent in. From then on I would get the boards, run them, and buy the prizes at stores in Danville. I was rolling in the money, not even considering that it was cheating and gambling, two activities strongly opposed by my Christian upbringing. I was never caught by the company. They never stopped sending me boards, so my coffers kept fattening.

We lived on the river and were the only family that had a cane patch. Some people call them bamboo or reeds, and they make great cane fishing poles. Reeds, being hollow, can also be used to make fantastic spitball shooters. Imagine a reed with a one-inch bore. In the right hands, a spitball shooter with a one-inch bore can pack quite a skin-reddening wallop.

My other moneymaking scheme involved these spitball shooters. I would make a spitball shooter and take it to school. The boys would see me using it and just have to have one. I took orders only with a cash deposit up front. After everyone who wanted one was supplied, I would tease them with a bigger one and repeat the process until I had reached the maximum caliber available from our reed patch. I then went super size by using large sumac bush sections for the tube. These shooters would need a large piece of newspaper to make a spitball. As the caliber of the spitballs grew, so did the potential for doing bodily harm. One of the boys made a huge blister on Nancy Evans's neck when he was shooting at another boy. The boy ducked, and the spitball hit Nancy, who showed the huge blister to the teacher. The principal was called in, and I was given a cease-and-desist order. I laid low for the remainder of the school year but resumed my arms dealing at the start of the next term.

One way I tried to make money was selling the *Grit* newspaper. *Grit* was a weekly paper that many boys sold to earn money. Boys in populated areas may have done well, but we were sparsely populated. There was too much distance between my potential customers, so I gave up on being a newspaper boy. The *Grit* was very popular at the time, which was partly due to the editorial policy of the paper. The stories were uplifting during depressing times.

The supervisor to whom I reported insisted that I memorize the *Grit's* written policy, which I still recall as follows: Always keep *Grit* from being pessimistic. Avoid printing those things that distort the minds of readers or make them feel at odds with the world. Avoid showing the wrong side of things or making people feel discontented. Do nothing that will encourage fear, worry or temptation. . . . Wherever possible, suggest peace and goodwill toward men. Give our readers courage and strength for their daily tasks. Put happy thoughts, cheer, and contentment into their hearts.

This kind of news is just what the post-Depression, war-weary folks of those times needed to hear.

I went into several other ventures to supplement my tobacco money. By the time we sold tobacco each fall, I had earned and saved enough money from my other business ventures that I did not need to use any of my tobacco money. I will never find the words to describe the thrill of getting my first tobacco money. Daddy got permission for me to miss school so I could go to with him and Mama to sell my tobacco. We sold it at the Piedmont Warehouse in Danville. Daddy and Mama took me to Security National Bank in Danville, and I opened a savings account. I continued to do all manner of things to earn money. I never touched my tobacco money for my basic needs until I enrolled in college at Virginia Tech in the fall of 1955.

As I grow older I realize more and more the many valuable lessons taught to me by my mama and daddy. They were the kind of lessons that stand the test of time. I wasn't wise enough to appreciate them as I should have back then, but somehow I think they knew how I would feel as I matured and gained my own understanding of life.

Summer of Discontent

Bill Cosby tells a story about taking a course in philosophy during his first year of college. He tried out his newfound knowledge on his grandmother one morning at breakfast. "Grandmother," he asked in a very thoughtful voice, "is this glass half empty, or is this glass half full?"

His grandmother replied in a dismissive tone, "It depends on whether you are filling the glass or if you are pouring it out. Eat your cereal."

I suppose all kids challenge their parents at some time during their formative years. This is particularly true of their teen years, when they suddenly become all wise and all knowing. In 1950, at thirteen going on forty—my summer of discontent and intellectual expansion—I was a bit fuzzy on only a few subjects. That's when I challenged my father to the brink.

In other stories I have told of my dad's work ethic. What I haven't told about is how he often did things the hard way. A neighbor once said that if my dad were to dig a well, he would try to start at the bottom. It sometimes seemed that in his zeal for doing manual labor, he did not consider an easier or more efficient way to accomplish the same results. This often conflicted with my lack of enthusiasm for manual labor. With my newly acquired wisdom, my first thought, when given a chore, was always to consider whether or not the assigned work should be done at all. Would my not doing the work be any detriment to humankind? My next thought was to ask whether or not the objective could be accomplished with less manual labor than doing it Dad's way? The feedback I got from Daddy usually was, "If you will buckle down and get started, you will be done with the work before you can come up with a way out of doing it." My dad, being genuinely wise, tolerated my challenges by allowing me to test my wings. However, I could see his patience wear thin at times.

One job we did on the farm was to cut the tops out of fully matured green corn just above the ear. We tied them in bundles of about twelve stalks each with binder twine, normally used to tie baled hay together. We would then tie about ten bundles together into so-called shocks and leave them in the field to dry. These shocks are often seen as store displays or used as yard art during Halloween. When green grass was no longer available, we kids would trek to the field no matter

the weather and bring these shocks to the pasture and feed them to the cows. I don't remember ever seeing a cow actually eat those cornstalks. Mostly they walked and crapped on them.

On one really cold, rainy winter day, Daddy dispatched me to bring corn shocks to the cows. My creativity burst forth, and without reservation I said, "Daddy, instead of bringing the corn to the cows so they can shit on it here, why don't we take the cows to the cornfield and let them shit on it there?" Uh-oh! The big "S" word. That was unintended. The "S" word eliminated any possible consideration of my brilliant idea. Dad didn't say a word. He was probably pleased that my slip of the tongue would quiet me down for awhile. Naturally I rushed to do my assigned chore and politely asked if there was anything else I could do.

I have an aside to this story. I grew up with two older uncles who were full of mischief. We had a neighbor, "Mean Calvin," who had a cornfield near us. He had no children at home, so he had to bring his own corn shocks from the field. Most winter days he would go to the field in the late afternoon to get a corn shock. He would walk by with the rustling shock of corn hanging over his shoulder. He had to pass by a heavily brushed area. My Uncle Hansford told me one day, "Mean Calvin is so deaf he can't hear hisself fart. Let's hide in the brush and set his corn on fire." So we did. Luckily, old Calvin felt the heat and smelled the smoke in time. It scared me up a wonderful scare. We waited for repercussions that never came.

I asked Uncle Hansford, "What if old Mean Calvin had caught on fire?"

Uncle Hansford said, "I would have stomped the fire out."

Uncle Hansford and I laid low for a bit after that. It is amazing how such an act will calm and quiet a kid down for awhile. Mean Calvin didn't know which one of us Bend kids did the deed, so all of us were under suspicion but left alone. This act started a cold war with old Calvin that ended in détente that lasted until I left the Bend.

In my opinion, there were many useless tasks performed on the farm. At one time or another, I debated most of them with my father to no avail. My dad always listened patiently to my propositions but generally did not delay completing the work his way. Daddy stopped cutting corn tops after we kids left home, proving that the whole point was a way to keep us busy—idle hands, you know! He once told me that he was afraid that I might grow up to become a lawyer.

Slowly my summer of discontent neared its end, laboriously for my dad. I could sense his excitement at my returning to school and restoring calm to his life. It wasn't to be. My daddy always planted far more of everything in our garden than we could ever consume. He would not let anything go to waste. We picked, gleaned, and harvested every bean, pea, green, fruit, or whatever was edible. We dried, canned, salted, jammed, preserved, and stored it all.

When school started in September, we farm kids were let out at noon until all the tobacco was in and the fall garden harvest was complete. There was nothing more distasteful to my sisters and me than to have to work upon our return from a school day. We wanted only to get home, eat a little food, and listen to radio station WREV. They broadcast a music program that took requests. Kids in the local schools would call in requests for songs to be played for their sweethearts or for someone who broke their hearts or to get even with someone.

On a hot, muggy September day, we got home from school and were assigned to go to a really large blackeyed pea field and pick all the peas that had not been harvested during the summer. These peas were to be picked and put into burlap bags. The bags would be tied at the top, and then we would jump up and down on them to crush the hulls from the peas. The peas and hulls were then poured out in a pile, and the peas were picked out from the hulls and stored for winter eating. That was a great deal of work, but kid labor had no recompense. (Dried peas soaked overnight and boiled in a little pork fat, salt, and pepper are hard to beat. We still buy them for a tasty winter meal. However, we do cheat by using olive oil instead of pork fat.)

It was really, really hot that day. I looked at the hot field and then looked at the shade of a nearby huge spreading oak tree. I had a great idea that became the straw that nearly broke the camel's back for my dad. Betty Jean, Elaine, Brenda, and I pulled the vines up and dragged them to the shade of the oak tree. We sat under the shade of that wonderful old tree and picked, stomped, and separated the peas from the chaff. As we were finishing up and darkness was creeping upon us, Daddy appeared. "What in the world is going on here?" I thought it was apparent and brilliant what was going on there, but not so my daddy. "LaVerne, this was your idea. You have been an aggravation to me this whole summer!"

My three sisters said in unison, "LaVerne made us do it."

"This antic is the crown jewel of your laziness. I wanted to leave the vines in the field to provide organic matter for the soil."

Somewhat quick on my feet, I replied, "We were just starting to put the vines back in the field when you came."

"That you will do, and you will do it alone," Dad said.

I did it in record time and rushed home for supper just as it was getting dark.

Things smoothed out for the remainder of the school year. The following year, at dried pea-picking time, Dad instructed us to pull the vines up and pick them in the shade. "Be sure you put the vines back in the field," he said as he drove away on his tractor. It took a year, but I had a sense of sweet victory. I, LaVerne Thornton, had actually taught my daddy, Perry James Thornton, how to do something in a better, easier way.

I became an engineer instead of a lawyer. Engineers work to simplify and take labor out of work, so finally my bright ideas got the attention they deserved.

I seemed to have had the answers to fewer and fewer questions as I grew older. Fortunately, Daddy grew smarter and wiser with time.

Skinny-Dipping

Before I tell you about our swimming hole and the culture that surrounded it, you should know the cast of characters. I, LaVerne, was not the youngest but the smallest of the group. I had no flaws, faults, or deficiencies whatsoever. I never did anything wrong. All the naughtiness herein discussed was planned and executed by others; I simply went along. I will not use the correct names of the swimming-hole group for fear that the statute of limitations may not have run out on some of our activities or that Mr. Doochie's heirs may want their plank back. I am using my own name because, as you may recall, I'm writing this story, and I want to be sure I get credit for it.

The oldest was Hermon. Hermon was tall and skinny for his age. He always looked like he stood too deep in his pants and too far up in his cap. Picture the waist of his pants up near his armpits and his cap down low enough to push his ears out. His cap sat square on his head. He never had well-fitting pants. They were always too large in the waist so when his belt was pulled tight, his pants gathered around his waist and left about thirteen inches of belt hanging down his side. His vocabulary consisted mainly of four words—yeah, nah, and f**k you. Not only did Hermon not know much, he didn't suspect much of anything either. Being extremely strong, Hermon was our barge, our motor grader, and our tow truck.

The youngest was Bobby. Bobby was fat with a red face and blondish hair that looked as if it had never been combed. He would spit when he talked and get overly excited in tense moments, such as sneaking onto other people's property. He would follow Hermon anywhere. He would also follow anyone else who had a candy bar. Bobby peed in his pants and puked occasionally.

James was shy, quiet, and rarely made suggestions but never failed to go along. James did plan one event. We all had Little Daisy, Red Ryder air rifles. One Sunday afternoon we were playing cowboys and Indians in the woods behind James's house. James suggested we take our clothes off, hide behind trees, and shoot at each other. Someone said, "Cowboys and Indians didn't go naked."

James said, "Indians did so, because Indians didn't have stores until the 'White Socks' came." We tried the game but abandoned it after only one shot was fired. Hermon shot Bobby's butt, which was sticking out from a tree too small for Bobby to hide behind. Bobby peed and puked on the tree. We never played that game again.

Sonny was a little younger than Hermon and was intelligent, strong, and quiet. He was my best friend among the group.

This group made up the core swimming-hole group. However, any number of boys could show up as visiting relatives or invited guests.

We all lived near the banks of the Dan River just two miles southwest of Danville, Virginia, as the crow flies, but about four miles by river. The mileage difference was due to the fact that the Dan River leaves North Carolina as shown on the map on page xiv, and carves a curvy semicircle into Virginia, encompassing around two thousand acres. The river then flows southward back into North Carolina and makes a hairpin turn northward back toward Danville, Virginia. This work of God left our family and twenty-nine other families isolated in the Bend by the river from the remainder of Virginia. The river was not particularly wide or deep. It contained an abundance of sewage from Leaksville, Draper, and Spray, North Carolina, which are now collectively known as Eden, North Carolina. We didn't know any better, so we swam in the river anyway.

It is one thing to wade in the river, but to dive and swim you need a really deep spot. This we found two farms north of my home. It was on Gauldin land. This is important because the last thing Mr. Gauldin wanted to see was kids having fun. Not being a particularly bright man, he finally gave up after we intimidated, outnumbered, and outsmarted him. We essentially took over his river bottom. Our swimming hole was great for skinny-dipping because it was completely isolated from society. The nearest road was three-quarters of a mile away and was dirt. The nearest house was one-half mile away through thick woods. The spot was made deep by a rock formation that stuck out into the river, forming a kind of dam. On the bank was a huge sycamore tree. Over the years the river had undercut the root system, causing the tree to lean into the river at about a thirty-degree angle. To add the crème de la crème, there was a huge grapevine rooted just so at the base of the tree, and it wound its way far up into the branches. It was sent from God. I never dreamed of such a gift from God. I felt exonerated from all my sins: feeding goat turds to Ann Hunt, rolling Helen Overby down the hill in a tractor tire, peeping at the sinners during revival, and so on.

During the winter we prepared our swimming hole for summer. We cut the grapevine off at the base and had Hermon climb up and cut the vine from the grip it held on the tree as it wound its way around and up. The long, skinny branches at the top were left to provide a strong attachment for the vine. The vine then swung free. Hermon was afraid to come down from the sycamore. We spent a long while coaxing him to come down the way he went up. Finally, someone said, "Just shimmy down the vine." Hermon never gave a thought to being fully clothed; halfway down he lost his grip and plunged into the deepest part of the half-frozen river. He stayed down longer than we expected.

We reacted as always in a crisis. We screamed and cried, "Hermon is dead! Hermon is dead!" Bobby peed in his pants and puked. Our concept of time was very poor. Hermon came up laughing hysterically.

We didn't wait for summer. In April our fun began! One boy would take a long pole and nudge the vine to the bank. Whoever had the next turn would hold on to the vine and swing way out over the river and drop off. I don't think it's possible to have more fun.

Never content to leave well enough alone, we wanted a diving board. This desire at first seemed impossible. It took awhile, but we finally came up with a solution.

As I said earlier, we lived in a very isolated place. There was only one dirt road; it left North Carolina, went eight-tenths of a mile into Virginia, and dead-ended. This provided a perfect location to make bootleg liquor, and make liquor they did. We had a local bootlegger named Doochie. Doochie had a tobacco barn just over the state line in North Carolina, which was in sight of a barn belonging to Sonny's family. This particular summer, Sonny and I decided not to sleep in a bed from the day school let out until the first day of the new school year. I could never explain just how much freedom that can give a kid. All we had to do was show up for farmwork early every morning. On one occasion we were sleeping in Sonny's barn. At about 3:30 a.m., we saw a 1940 Ford coupe stop at Doochie's barn. We were terribly afraid but more curious than afraid. We crept through the woods to get a good look at what was going on. We saw the driver lift several long, wide boards from a stack of lumber that seemed always to be there. He then placed four large boxes into the center of the stack of lumber just as if there was a large hole in the middle of the stack. When the driver finished offloading, I swear the back of that Ford coupe raised up two feet. All of us local boys knew what this souped-up car was. The driver was Peg Crowder, a local whiskey runner, who had a peg leg. These whiskey haulers were the forerunners of today's NASCAR drivers.

After the driver left, we got up the nerve to check out the lumber stack. We found it was a clever way of hiding cases of liquor. The lumber stack was made up of long pieces of lumber on the outside and short boards on each end of the middle. This arrangement was topped off with long, wide boards all across the top. The driver restacked the pile, and one would never suspect that there was stuff hidden in there. *Ooh la la!* Did you hear what I said? The stuff was covered with oodles of long, wide boards—long, wide *diving* boards.

How do you acquire one of Mr. Doochie's long, wide boards? You don't walk up and say, "Mr. Doochie, may we have one of those wide boards you use to hide your liquor with?" You can't buy one because you have no money. What you do over a week's time is to convince yourselves that taking a board from a bootlegger is not stealing. Problem solved. We stayed at Sonny's barn nightly until we figured out Mr. Doochie's MO. Mr. Doochie apparently laid low for a time after he received a load in case Mr. Peg had been followed. He would then relocate his wares. We waited until he relocated his whiskey. After he had been gone for awhile, we moved in and in a flash we reallocated the best-looking board to a place deep in the woods. Each night we would move the board closer to the river. Finally, we got the board to our swimming hole about two miles away. After thinking about the sin we had committed, I puked, Bobby peed in his pants, and all the others except Hermon cried. Hermon didn't mind that we had committed the sin of stealing. He just lit a cigarette and grinned. We soon got over our guilt and proceeded with our plans.

Now we needed posts. Mr. Graham owned the farm adjacent to us. We were allowed to use a path through his property as a shortcut to our mailbox. We lived in Virginia, and our mail could only be brought to a spot on the North Carolina line about one-half mile from our house. Several of us kids were expected to be seen on that path. I had noticed that Mr. Graham was putting up a fence. He had really big, round locust posts for his corners. You know where this is going. We boys thought long and hard to excuse ourselves for "borrowing" two of those posts. Thankfully, we remembered that Mr. Graham once cursed us and told us to get the hell out of his orchard. That gave us the excuse we needed. We used the same clandestine way we had exercised to relocate our big, wide, thick board from Mr. Doochie. A few scrap boards, a few nails, and some tools put us in business.

For variety and excitement we found some long-fallen trees, sawed the limbs off close to the trunk, and cut them into about eight-foot lengths. We put them in the river, sat on one end, and floated. Well, floating is more fun the farther you float. So, one Sunday afternoon four of us decided to float way down the river. We had to push the logs over some places, but mostly we could float. We were having so much fun that we lost track of how far we had gone. Now, as the river approached Danville, there was a hydroelectric dam that was used to make electricity for Dan River Mills. The river was deep enough and wide enough for motorboats. We suddenly realized that there we were—four naked boys fast approaching a large crowd of people and surrounded by motorboats. We were in deep water by now. We abandoned our logs and swam for the bank. Then, by crawling, wading, and swimming, we got back to our swimming hole. That was a long, hard, time-consuming ordeal. From that day on, we stuck close to our swimming hole.

There were no phones, so there was no way to let each other know specific times to meet at the swimming hole. We simply knew when to show up. As we arrived at the river, we would

strip our clothes off, put them on our designated rock, and jump right in. This was how it was for a few years—a giggling group of naked boys without a care in the world.

We all tried smoking at the swimming hole. Hermon rolled his own, so he furnished the papers. We all sneaked some dried tobacco from our barns. We crushed it really fine and rolled it into crude cigarettes. Bobby and I puked after about three puffs. James cried and said that his mother would kill him when he got home. Hermon said that he chewed pine needles, and his mother had never noticed that he had been smoking. Adopting this idea, we all chewed pine needles.

When I got home, my mother never looked up from her sewing. She said, "You have been smoking because I smell pine needles." That's all she said.

I suppose that when she did look up and saw my green complexion, she assumed that I had cured myself of smoking.

That old swimming hole was our main source of pleasure for several years, but as they say, all good things must come to an end. The demise of our group started when puberty struck. The older boys started to change. They combed their hair neater, wore better-fitting clothes, and looked at themselves in every mirror they passed. Voices started to change, and bodies filled out to match feet, ears, and hands.

On one of the first days at the swimming hole for the summer, we all were there except Hermon. Soon he arrived, but he looked different; he swaggered. He had on tight-fitting Wranglers and a T-shirt with cigarettes wrapped in a twist in his shirt sleeve. It was sorta James Dean style. His body had filled out so that his feet, hands, and ears matched better. His usually unkempt hair was oiled down with Sure Lay hair tonic and styled in a ducktail. He lingered on the bank for awhile after everyone else was in the water. Slowly, Hermon started to undress. When he was stripped of his clothes, he strangely walked up and down the bank. By this time everyone had stared his way. Suddenly, we knew why his strange behavior was happening. No longer did he have a winkie or a goober. Over the winter the dude had grown a hammer. This revelation caused each of us to stay in the water the whole time, instead of repeatedly diving and jumping in the river as we usually did. Upon getting out of the river, each of us backed up to our clothes and got into them quickly, except for Hermon. Hermon dressed slowly and then showed us his rubber. Boy, did he proudly display that rubber. I never heard the word for rubber being "condom" until recently when some high schools started making them available to students.

I looked at it for awhile and then said, "Hermon, looks like your rubber is dry-rotted." That was the wrong thing to say. Hermon got so mad that he shoved me in the river and jumped in behind me. Both of us were fully clothed. I was by far the better swimmer and easily got to the other side of the river and outran him. Hermon's anger was soon forgotten, but after that day the old swimming hole was never quite the same.

How about Them Apples

I was recently in an antique shop in Williamsburg, Virginia, looking at all the things that I grew up with and used on the farm: butter churns, assorted hand tools, and so on. Soon I came across a machine that brought forth fond memories, nostalgic feelings, and a lump in my throat. I saw an old apple cider press. All the parts were there and functioning.

On the long drive from Williamsburg to my home in Sanford, North Carolina, I thought of all the ways that apples were a part of my childhood. Most of the farms in the Bend had orchards where a variety of fruits like plums, peaches, apples, pears, cherries, and so forth were grown. Also an array of vine-growing fruits were grown in the orchards, such as berries and grapes. We had a great orchard, only bested by Mr. Lacy Graham's orchard on the farm next to us. We boys called him "Mr. Lacy" and found his orchard irresistible. It was what lawyers call an "attractive nuisance." Mr. Lacy's land was divided by the North Carolina and Virginia state line, and his house was the last one on the North Carolina side of the one dirt road serving the Bend. The U.S. mail service stopped at his farm, and all the mailboxes for us Bend people were lined up along Gravel Hill Road at the end of his driveway on the North Carolina side. Most of the time we all walked to the mailboxes to get our mail. We would sometimes pick up neighbors' mail and deliver it to them. It was an unwritten rule in the Bend that "convenience paths" were allowed across one's property. Such a path was used as a shortcut across Mr. Lacy's farm from the Bend homes to the mailboxes. This path conveniently passed through Mr. Lacy's orchard. This easy access allowed for more fruit stealing from Mr. Lacy's orchard than takes place on a New Jersey shipping dock. Mr. Lacy was considerably older than his wife, and they had one child, a baby girl. There was no one to avoid while on their property except for Mr. Lacy and his wife.

Mr. Lacy had more tools than anyone else in the Bend. We boys knew everyone's schedule in the Bend, all of their goings and comings. We used this knowledge to borrow whatever tools we needed for our ventures. In defense of our borrowing policy, it did allow us to acquire skills that we may not have learned otherwise. My dad asked me once, "LaVerne, how did you learn to use a planing tool so well?"

I had the typical child's response, "I don'know." Actually, I learned by using Mr. Lacy's planing tool to work on a diving board that we stole from Doochie, a local bootlegger.

One early fall day after school had started, when apples were plentiful and ripe, Sonny, Hermon, James, Bobby, and I decided to make apple cider using Mr. Lacy's apples and his cider press. We planned everything out to perfection. We knew the day when Mr. Lacy took his wife to visit some relative in Pelham, North Carolina, for a full afternoon and returned normally after dark. After school on one of those days, we each slipped some canning jars from our mothers' storage places. Since it was near the end of canning season, this was a little difficult, but we got enough to go through with our plan. We gathered at Mr. Lacy's shed where he had his cider press mounted. Our plan was for Bobby and James to take a bushel basket to the orchard and bring it back full of apples, drop the full basket off, and take an empty one back to the orchard for more apples. The rest of us would be setting up the press. Hermon was to put apples in the cider press tub. Sonny would wind the cider press platen down to squeeze the juice out, and I was to catch the juice in the jars and put on the lids. Sonny and Hermon would

then remove the pulp from the press and refill it with a fresh batch of apples. We planned to press out about ten half-gallon jars of juice. We figured that would be as much as we could escape with—two jars each for five of us. One of us would stay back to dispose of the apple pulp, clean up, and remove all signs that we had been there.

All was going well. We would be finished before Mr. Lacy got back, according to our calculations. Suddenly around the corner came Mr. Lacy. He was a large, imposing man who shaved maybe monthly. He had a snarl on his face that would melt steel. We were much too scared to run, so we were frozen in place. At moments like this I always imagined jail and how old I would be if I escaped or were released on parole. I had heard the old radio program *The FBI* on our battery-operated Philco radio. I was aware that crossing a state line to commit a crime made it a federal offense. Mr. Lacy's cider press was in North Carolina; we lived in Virginia. My short life passed in front of my eyes. Bobby was peeing in his pants and puking. Hermon looked like a stone statue, motionless and emotionless. James was crying, and Sonny spilled a bushel of apple pulp at Mr. Lacy's feet. It seemed an eternity before Mr. Lacy said a word. It was enough time for me to ask God for forgiveness for all the bad things that I had ever done.

Finally Mr. Lacy spoke. He said, "Boys, I could get the law after you, but I won't." Thank God; I got some relief. He continued, "I won't even tell your parents. No, you need to learn a real lesson. I have a chance to sell one hundred gallons of fresh cider to the Old Dutch Super-market in Danville. I was going to turn it down, but now that I have plenty of help, I think I will accept that offer. Starting tomorrow, you boys are going to help me make one hundred gallons of cider." Anything short of reporting us to the sheriff or telling our parents was a real relief; besides, we weren't given a choice.

Mr. Lacy then asked, "Did you boys clean that press before you started?"

We answered, "No . . ."

"Did you wash the apples real good before you pressed them?"

"No . . ."

"Did you pick out the ones that may have worms in them?"

"No . . ."

"Did you carefully pick out the ones that had rotten spots on them?"

"No . . ."

"Did you cut the apples off the core?"

"No . . ."

"Well, you will from now on! Before each use, you must disassemble the press and wash it in warm, soapy water. You can get the warm water and soap at my house. You must pick through the apples and wash them in soap and water and rinse them twice in clear water. I will bring the tubs and water and will have the gallon jugs. I know you can be here after school each day—I'll see you tomorrow." As Mr. Lacy was leaving, he turned and said, "I wouldn't drink that cider; it probably has worms, insect droppings, spider eggs, and bird shit in it, as well as the insecticide that I spray on the trees."

Fresh, clean canning jars were put back into our moms' storage places that very day. All that planning and work was for naught.

On the way home, we talked about what to tell our mothers and dads. How could we explain why we were going to help Mr. Lacy make cider? Anyway, how the heck long would it take to make a hundred gallons of cider the way Mr. Lacy was requiring us to do it? We settled on what to tell our parents.

When I got home, Mama asked, "Where have you been? You are late."

I replied sheepishly, "Mr. Lacy was showing us boys how to make cider. You know Mama, Mr. Lacy is getting old, and he has to make a great quantity of cider to sell. He probably needs the money. We are going to help him make that cider."

Mama hugged me tight and said, "Son, you are such a sensitive and caring child."

The first day at our cider-making punishment, Mr. Lacy was all set up. He had three tubs and plenty of water. He went to the orchard with us and showed us how to grade the apples. Also, he helped us wash and rinse them. We placed the apples on a clean bedsheet. He had knives for all of us and showed us how to cut four large pieces off the apples leaving square cores. He explained that leaving a large core wasn't a waste because he had far more apples than needed, and besides that, he would feed the apple cores to his hogs.

Mr. Lacy told us a funny story. He said that you have to be careful to feed the apple cores to the hogs while they were fresh. One time he overlooked a bucket of cores for about a week but fed them to his hogs anyway. The hogs went sort of wild, stumbling into one another and running into the fence. Turned out, he said, that the apple cores had fermented and the hogs were drunk. He added, "Those hogs seemed to be dissatisfied with the next batch of cores I gave them."

The next day we could hardly wait to get to Mr. Lacy's place. We worked like well-experienced cider makers, laughing as we worked and chiding anyone who slacked off the least bit. Mr. Lacy made each one of us perform every task until we could do it well. He seemed to enjoy the experience as much as anyone. Making the cider became a social thing for us. We gave our parents enthusiastic reports each day. However, the amount of cider we were producing was going really slowly. We figured it would take several weeks to make that one hundred gallons, but we didn't worry; we were having fun.

After one week, Mr. Lacy announced that Old Dutch had canceled its order and that we had probably learned our lesson anyway. He gave each of us a gallon of cider to take home. I wondered about that Old Dutch story after that. I was with Uncle Luther and Aunt Duddy in the Old Dutch Supermarket in Danville several times, and I never saw any gallons of cider.

Mama came home from Mr. Walter Smart's store one day and said, "I saw Mr. Lacy at the store today."

I thought, *Oh, no, here it comes.*

"He told me how much he enjoyed and appreciated you boys helping him make cider, and that if he had a son, he would like for him to be just like you."

After our cider-making punishment, you could often find us boys hanging out with Mr. Lacy. He would show us how to use tools. He would let us sharpen our pocket knives on his pedal-driven whet rock, bore a hole in wood on his pedal-driven drill press, or turn a homemade baseball bat on his gasoline-powered wood lathe.

I went to see Mr. Lacy for the last time a few months after I finished college. He seemed truly glad to see me. With a big grin and twinkling eyes, he gave me a large bag of apples since it was fall again and cider-making time.

Tall Cotton Silk Stilts

I was with Daddy at Mr. Walter Smart's store one cold, rainy day in winter. There were several menfolk sitting on nail kegs around the potbellied coal stove, talking. I loved to blend into the background on these occasions and hear all the man talk. They would get excited and forget that I was around and take no care of what they talked about. Several of these men never worked. They were large landowners on the North Carolina side of the state line and were reputed to own stock, a rare thing around there. Sometimes on a rainy day, there was a tenant farmer named Mr. Crowder listening in on the conversation. I say listening because he rarely talked much. Though he was a poor tenant farmer, he was considered wise to the point that even those wealthy men called him "Mr. Crowder." On this particular morning Mr. Crowder was present. He was sitting on his nail keg with his head in its usual pose that made him appear to be staring at the floor. There were no women present, and I was partially hidden and forgotten. The conversation turned to how many times each man had sex on their first night of marriage. Several men stated from two to five times.

Finally, Mr. Stacy said, "Mr. Crowder, you haven't told us how many times you had sex on your first night of marriage."

Without looking up, Mr. Crowder said in a slow drawl, "Just once. Becky won't used to it."

The talk went on for awhile, and I soaked up all that wonderful stuff that I could go back to the Bend and tell my buddies. Then an event took place that altered my and my buddies' conversations. Witcher Eanes, home from being wounded in World War II, drove up in a brand-new, 1946 Ford coupe. That car was shiny black and jacked up in the back, bootlegger style. It was loaded with every extra that could be hung on a car, including a sun visor, curb finders, spotlights, fog lights, and fender skirts. He even had a foxtail hanging from the rearview mirror. Witcher was wearing white shoes, white duck pants, a pale blue shirt, and a navy sport coat. He swaggered into the store under everyone's gaze. Mr. Walter Smart stared at him and said, "Boy, you are shitn' in tall cotton, ain't cha?" I thought that was the most beautiful way to string words together that I had ever heard. I didn't know exactly what it meant or from where it evolved; I only knew that it was like music to me. I have loved country expressions ever since. I knew that expression must describe someone at the top of his game.

From the time I told my Bend buddies that story, that expression became a constant part of our conversation. Do a neat trick on your bike, and you were "shitn' in tall cotton." I made straight A's on my report card. I was "shitn' in tall cotton." "Shitn' in tall cotton" became something to achieve in everything we did. It was our goal, our theme, and our aim to be "shitn' in tall cotton," whatever the activity.

We wore those words out until an event Hermon was involved in brought us a new expression.

We Bend boys did everything to excess until someone got hurt or was brought back to earth by a parent or until a group of parents issued a cease-and-desist order. For instance, we made our own slingshots. We would go into the forest and search out a sapling that grew with a forked branch. Then we would cut the fork off and trim it into a Y pattern. An old inner tube in 1940s car tires was used for the rubbers. A leather shoe tongue was trimmed for the rock pocket. Add a few inches of twine, and you had all the materials for a slingshot. Well, we each had to get bigger and better. We escalated the size and power of slingshots to the point that we could do serious damage, and damage we did. We could be aiming for a target and hit a car or truck instead. In a moment of stupidity or by accident, someone might hit a farm animal—not to harm them, of course, but we often did. We even built a four-man slingshot. Two held the forks and aimed while two boys pulled back the rock pocket. We could cast a larger rock but never got the aiming thing down.

The same story goes for homemade bows. Bows got bigger and bigger, and arrows got longer, stronger, and sharper. Authentic Indian arrowheads could be found everywhere in the Bend, especially along the river. We would fit the real Indian arrowheads to our arrows. We made a catapult with stolen—I mean borrowed—materials from Mr. Lacy Graham's farm and those dependable rubber inner tubes. We could throw a two-pound rock for a long distance but had no control over where it landed. We would often wind up with weapons with which you could go to war. All this work and competition so we could lay claim to "shitn' in tall cotton."

I think that making our own toys helped me to prepare for my engineering career.

One day Hermon, James, and I hitched a ride to Danville. Sonny had to work, and Bobby couldn't be found. We had new heel taps on our shoes and wore our cleanest blue jeans with the cuffs turned up as was the style in the late forties. We oiled our hair with Sure Lay hair tonic. Our plans were to hang out at a poolroom since we believed that to be a rite of passage for hip young men. We were in the pool hall about a New York minute before we were thrown out. We wandered over to Main Street and found a good place to lean against a wall, spit on the sidewalk, and generally look cool. While we were standing there, a mother and her young daughter passed by. The little girl had on a frilly dress, a bow in her hair, and black patent-leather shoes with lace socks. Mom was equally well-dressed. As they moved by with a look of disdain toward us, Hermon said in his country, hick voice, "That girl right dere poots through silk." "Shitn' in tall cotton" no longer was the only expression used to describe someone at the top of his or her game; it was "pootn' through silk" from then on.

We took up tom walkers one summer. I don't know who in the Bend introduced tom walkers, known by some people as stilts. We took tom walkers on like all other fads. Taller and higher is the only way tom walking can escalate. So escalate it did. About midsummer none of us had reached "shitn' in tall cotton" status, but we were trying. Availability of materials was a problem.

All of us except Bobby were hanging out by a tobacco barn adjacent to Gravel Hill Road on a really hot day. We were wondering where Bobby had been lately. We heard a *thump, thump, thump,* and here comes Bobby on the tallest pair of tom walkers we had ever seen. Bobby had achieved "shitn' in tall cotton" less often than any of us, so it was a thrill to see him being an obvious winner. Turns out he had an uncle who worked at a lumber yard. Bobby's uncle had furnished him material to make those tall tom walkers. We learned that Bobby had mounted the tall walkers by standing on a really high porch railing at his house. As he approached, he was red-faced tired, spitting as usual, and shouting loudly, "I'm shitn' in tall cotton and pootn' through silk!"

It is really hard to stand still on a tom walker. You need to shift constantly to maintain balance. So Bobby, totally exhausted by now, was shifting about and saying, "Help me down. I got to pee." He was afraid to get down, and we didn't aim to help. We thought ourselves too old to cry, but Bobby started to cry and beg. The tears flowed and soon the pee. Pee ran down his leg and on down those giant tom walkers, so we broke down and helped him off. Since we felt bad for him and a bit ashamed of our behavior, we voted him the permanent "pootn' through silk" world champion award.

The Fart Heard All over Pittsylvania County

When I was about ten years old, I would occasionally visit my three cousins—Joanne, Teeny, and Charles Kepley—in Gretna, Virginia, which is in Pittsylvania County. Uncle Crawford fox hunted with a group of local farmers. I'm not talking about dressing in fancy riding clothes, turning a fox loose, and carrying a tiny flask of brandy on your hip. I'm talking about truckloads of hounds in rusty pickup trucks and passing around a fruit jar full of moonshine—that kind of fox hunting. I loved to go fox hunting with Uncle Crawford. There was a good deal of creative cussing, tobacco chewing, and dirty-joke telling. I wasn't allowed to use those words, but I filed them away in my brain for when I grew up.

On one of these trips I was to go fox hunting with Uncle Crawford. Charles was too young to go with us, so that made me feel special. We were to drop Aunt C.D. and the three kids off at a fox hunter's home before we met the other hunters. When we got to the home, I saw in the yard the most beautiful girl I had ever seen. She had black hair and the prettiest brown eyes. I was smitten and got my first tingle in my growing area. I was glad that I had on my new Red Ball tennis shoes and my Levi's with the cuffs turned up. With those new Red Balls on, I felt that I could run faster and jump higher than anybody. I couldn't see leaving that pretty girl to go fox hunting. I told Uncle Crawford that I didn't feel well, so I was going to stay back and play with the girls. He paid little attention to my excuse, so all was going well. Soon the girls drew a hopscotch pattern on the ground. (You can find a wonderful description of hopscotch on Google.) When playing hopscotch, your marker is very important. Most kids used a piece of colorful broken glass. You strive to have something unique. Well, this little girl had the most unique marker that she kept in a velvet drawstring pouch. Her marker was a shiny, silvery, butterscotch-colored piece of glass that changed colors as you moved it about. I later learned that it was known as carnival glass. It was usually given as a prize, in the form of dinnerware, at the county fair. The girls asked me to play, but I could not play such a sissy game while wooing a girl. I had a bigger plan.

Just as they finished a game and before they started a new one, I was going to demonstrate how fast I could run and how high I could jump. I've since seen Ernest T. Bass do this on

the *Andy Griffith Show*. I got up to full speed, and just as I got to the edge of the hopscotch diagram I left the ground. As I reached the height of my arc, I farted—not a little-boy poot, but a man-sized, bun-flapper, ending-with-a-whistling-fizzle kind of fart. Needless to say, I could not stop and face the object of my affection after that event. I never broke stride when I hit the ground, but kept running until I was deep in the forest. I hid behind a big poplar tree until I got my breath and started to make a plan. I fully intended to stay in those woods until I grew a beard or was drafted into the army. I don't know how long I stayed hidden, but eventually Uncle Crawford had the fox hounds track me down. Aunt C.D. probably saved me from embarrassment because all the people were in the house when we came out of the woods.

I eventually married a beautiful black-haired girl with the prettiest brown eyes. I don't think she is the same girl, but I was just as smitten by her at first sight. I got that same tingle in the growing area.

Sex in the Bend

Working hard on the farm and swimming regularly in the Dan River made me tough and strong for such a little kid. I was never good at athletics. I might have been if I had been given the chance. My father was a high school baseball star. He was one of the few men in the Bend who finished high school. My dad later played semipro baseball with a Danville, Virginia, team. We lived too far from Happy Home Elementary School and even farther away from Ruffin High School for me to participate in sports. I excelled at two things: swimming and cutting monkey shines. We boys would spend entire Sunday afternoons in a thick-forested area of the Bend swinging from tree to tree like monkeys. We went for distance. The one who could traverse the greatest distance from the starting place without touching the ground was the winner. I won most of the time through a combination of skill, raw guts, and pure stupidity. Climbing and swimming were my skills, and climbing trees was by far my best skill. If the Olympic Games had swinging from trees for distance in their events, I believe that I could easily make the U.S.A. team for the next Summer Olympic Games in England in 2012, even at my advanced age. All the kids knew of my skills, particularly the girls. Around the time I was deep into puberty, I went to considerable effort to keep them reminded.

With a hair or two on our chins and changing voices, we boys were entertaining some girls one day on the playground during recess. We were trying to keep our voices in the low-pitch mode. There was an aluminum flagpole standing there begging to be climbed. Several boys attempted to climb it. After getting up between four and six feet, they all slid down. One of the girls whom I was extremely interested in impressing said, "I bet LaVerne can climb it."

I doubted my skills and said abruptly and loudly, "Recess is over!"

Then James the spoiler said, "I double-dog dare you." You can get by not responding to a double-dog dare if only boys are around, but in front of a girl you are toast if you don't respond to a double-dog dare.

I was trembling with fear and doubt as I approached the flagpole. I slid my hand up and down the pole, which was by now, with the other boys' attempts to climb it, slick as eel shit. I couldn't stop now. My only hope was to get higher than anyone else had. Getting a little higher

than the other boys would save face. I gripped the pole with all my strength as high up as I could reach, lifted my body up, and quickly gripped the pole between my knees as tightly as my quivering legs could bear. I was making progress and gained about a foot. I repeated the procedure several times to the cheers of the kids. I did pay enough attention to know that Bernice Eanes was cheering. Needing only one more lurch to reach the top, I prayed for the recess bell to save me since I was totally exhausted. No bell. I made a final lunge, gripping tighter than ever with my hands and then my knees. As I attempted to tighten my knees on the pole, a strange feeling took place in my groin. I lost control just as the bell rang and slid down that pole at the speed of sound. My first thought was, *I have busted that gut Mama always threatened me about*. No one really noticed my rapid descent and my rush away from the pole. All the kids knew about my being under orders to be promptly in my seat after recess. I had probably hundreds of entries in my permanent record by now for being late into my seat after recess. (My permanent record was a subject that we have already examined in a previous story.)

The more I thought about that flagpole incident, and after enough time to realize no permanent damage had been done, I thought that was really a pleasant thing that happened at the top of that pole. I wondered if I could make it happen again. The more I thought about it, the more I would like to experience it again—not on that flagpole though. I won once; no need risking failure with a second try. I quit flagpole climbing at the top of my game and with a legendary reputation in the Bend.

After leaving the episode behind me for a few days, I started to notice the empty haystack pole down near the barn. I am sure that you have all seen one in pictures of a pastoral farm scene. It is usually a straight cedar pole about ten inches in diameter planted with the big end in the ground so it sticks straight up about thirty feet in the air. Before baling came in use, hay was hauled from the hayfield by horse- or mule-drawn wagon. Pitchforks were used to pitch the hay evenly around the pole. We kids were assigned to walk the hay down to compact it as it was built up around the pole. This was my favorite job on the farm. When topped off, a used truck tire was placed around the pole on top of the hay. This tire placement would further compact and stabilize the hay. I couldn't stop wondering if that thing would happen if I climbed that haystack pole the same way I did the flagpole. Years of use and time had left it slick. I climbed up and slid down and climbed to the top—nothing; I slid down and climbed it again—nothing.

Mama shouted from the backyard, "Son, what on earth are you doing?"

"Just seeing how many times I can climb to the top of this ol' pole, Mama."

"Well, if you aren't careful, you are going to bust a gut."

I pretty much forgot about poles and strange sensations in my groin until one night at a birthday party. We Bend kids were allowed to have parties on our own without adult supervision.

We only played hopscotch, gossip, red rover, kick the can, and other children's games. It was becoming a different thing now. Some of us kids were either entering puberty or well into it. While the adults were preoccupied with corn shuckings, hog killings, wheat thrashings, and other community affairs, we boys were starting to prefer hiding with the girls when playing hide-and-seek. You would often hear a slap and then see a girl run from the hiding place followed by one of the boys with a red face. Bend-style sex education was getting into full swing.

These were the days before teachers rolled condoms on bananas to show kids how to have sex in order to keep them from wanting to have sex. Also, it was before a few deviant teachers bypassed the banana scene and went straight to free home demonstrations with students. Sex education was pretty much left for the kids to sort out for themselves as it had always been. In cavemen days, I doubt that Grog awakened one morning with a boner and ran to his mom and shouted, "See Grog got? What Grog do?" Grog knew what do. Grog had just dreamed about that little blond girl Pebble three caves up the hollow who had recently started filling out her leopard-skin wrap really well. Grog sneaked out of the cave before his parents got up from rock and headed three caves up the hollow. There he waited until Pebble went to the outrock. As she left the outrock completely relieved, he grabbed her. He dragged her to the nearby cave that was recently vacated by a family that had been supper for a saber-toothed tiger a moon ago. There he knew exactly what Grog do.

Attitudes toward sex by us Bend boys had only been civilized a bit since Grog. When it came to civilized sex, we were about like the third man from the left on the evolution chart who hadn't yet mastered that stand-erect thing. Sex education consisted of mothers telling sons, "Don't pick on girls; you know what I mean," and mothers telling their daughters, "Don't let boys pick on you; you know what I mean." The rest was left to us and nature. The boys tried to pick on girls just as they were told not to, and girls kept the boys at a distance most of the time.

I will return to the birthday party. It was summer, and I had spent a few days with my cousin in Danville. I came home a much more sophisticated young man, having been exposed to city life. While there, I went with my cousin to a party one night. Both my cousin's parents worked the night shift at Dan River Mills, as well as a bunch of his friends' parents. This left kids to do about what they pleased 'til midnight. At the party they played a game I knew straightaway I was going to like. It was called "spin the bottle." The game begins with the girls and boys sitting in a circle facing each other. A Pepsi bottle is placed in the middle of the circle, and someone is chosen to go first. This person is usually the oldest or toughest boy. The lucky boy spins the bottle. When the bottle stops spinning and it is pointing to a girl, she must go into a dark room and let the boy kiss her. Then she spins, following the same rules as the boys. If a boy spins and

the bottle stops and is pointing to a boy, that second boy gets to spin next. I was too shy to participate at that party. I did vow to myself to introduce that fantastic game to the Bend kids.

The time to introduce spin the bottle to the Bend kids came in the fall during Mr. Hazelwood's corn shucking. Back then, farmers raised feed corn for the farm animals. The corn was pulled off the stalk in the early fall after it had fully dried. As the corn was pulled off the stalk, it was pitched to a pile in the field. These piles were then gathered up, loaded on a mule-drawn wagon, and taken to a spot near the corncrib, a building where the corn was stored for winter feeding. These piles were formed in a row so neighbor men could sit on stools on the opposite side from the corncrib. They would gather at night, shuck the corn, and throw the ears into the crib. In the next few days, we kids would gather the ears of corn that missed getting into the crib and "throw them home," which meant the same as throwing them in the crib. In addition to being a work night for the men, corn shuckings were social events for all. The women would prepare a huge meal at supper for the event. These meals would often be an informal cooking competition among the women.

After supper on the day of Mr. Hazelwood's corn shucking, we kids left to go to another kid's house to celebrate Tiny Hyler's thirteenth birthday. After awhile, I suggested that we play spin the bottle. Some of the kids knew about the game and giggled. Finally we all decided to play. Someone got a bottle, and we formed the traditional ring. The game moved along with kids going into a dark bedroom. You could hear an occasional slap, some groping, and giggling. The boys would come out grinning, and the girls would be blushing. All these sights and sounds were to the raucous applause of everyone else. Finally, after it appeared that I was going to be left out, I got a turn. Tony Murphy's spin pointed to me. I was shaking like a leaf as I spun that Pepsi bottle while praying, *Please, God, let it stop on a girl with boobs; please let it stop on a girl with boobs*. It did. The bottle stopped dead to point on Hylda Stump. Now Hylda didn't look like much on the hoof, but she had the biggest boobs. She was also a bit on the chubby side and had freckles. But not to worry, it was dark in the room we went into, and as they say, "All cats are gray in the dark." I don't think either one of us was experienced, but we gave it our all. Hylda was willing and held that kiss a long time. Hello, hello! That groin thing happened. Unfortunately, the bottle never stopped on my favorite, Bernice Eanes.

If Hylda is alive today, she probably still wonders what was going on when I shouted, "You're better'n a flagpole!"

Sowing Wild Oats

Hermon, Sonny, James, Bobby, and I reached that age. You know the age I am talking about. A little chin hair started to sprout, and our voices often cracked when we spoke. We began to groom our hair better and even on occasions would sneak a little of our fathers' after-shave lotions. We noticed ourselves in every reflective surface from mirrors to shop windows to shiny car fenders. We wore heel taps on our shoes. Heel taps are small pieces of metal nailed to shoe heels so a loud tapping sound comes from each step made on wood floors and concrete walkways. They were fifties "cool." We had learned to wear our "privates" on the side of our tight blue jeans that would yield the biggest crotch bulge. The bulge was also checked often in any reflective surface. To be really cool you had to cup your bulge in one hand and hunch it up occasionally. This was a 1950s mating dance. We had begun to ignore one another often in favor of talking to girls. As our mothers would say, we were "feeling our oats."

We were not yet men, but we were outgrowing those devilish games we had so often played.

Many times we had crawled on our bellies in the woods to a spot where we could hide and watch the bootleggers make whiskey. We started to wonder what it would be like to get drunk. First we joked about it, but the subject began to come up more often. One day Hermon said, "Let's stop talking about getting drunk and do it."

At first we all said, "Not me," but we kept the subject alive. Anyway, where would we get the liquor? We had heard all our lives that some kids were caught spying on a bootlegger. He caught them and burned them in his liquor still fire. Believing that story made our spying on the bootleggers even more exciting, but eliminated stealing liquor from them as an option.

We talked about getting drunk until it became an obsession. The act of pulling it off without getting caught became more important than the actual act of getting drunk. We had clandestine meetings at the swimming hole. We put as much planning into getting drunk as Gen. Eisenhower did in planning D-Day. We didn't have to plan so much when we decided to cuss. We just met at the swimming hole one day and decided to start cussing. I knew the most words because of fox hunting with Uncle Crawford and listening to Uncle Luther and Aunt Duddy fight.

Finally, we hit upon a plan. Corn shuckings would take place in late September. Corn shuckings were a combination of work events and social gatherings. When the corn raised to feed the farm animals had dried on the stalk, farmers would gather the ears of corn and bring them in. The corn was placed in a long windrow in front of the corncrib. A group of about fourteen farmers in the Bend would get together and shuck each other's corn. On corn-shucking day, the host farmer's wife would prepare a tremendous evening country meal for the husbands and wives of the visiting shucking team. The women strutted their stuff at these events, using personal recipes that they would not dare share with anyone. One woman had her famous secret recipe carved on her gravestone. For years she had told everyone that they would get her recipe over her dead body.

After the meal the men would go out to the pile of corn and shuck it, throwing the ears into the crib where they were stored for feeding chickens, hogs, cows, and mules. Some of the corn was taken to the grist mill where it was ground into corn meal for making cornbread. The women joined together to clean up from the meal and then sat to knit, quilt, or just dip snuff and gossip. We boys would play a game of seeing who could stand in the path of the pitched corn the longest. This always resulted in head knots and assorted cuts and bruises.

We boys had observed through the years that on the day of the host farmer's shucking, the farmer would place several fruit jars filled with something besides fruit, if you know what I mean, in the corn pile. The jars were randomly placed at varying depths in the pile. The idea was that as the shuckers worked the pile down, they would find the jar of whiskey, whereupon they would pass it around. A quart jar per discovery was usually the amount. About four jars per shucking would last until the last ear of corn was shucked.

Our plan was to take our "getting drunk" liquor from the corn pile. Each of us would set aside two pint-sized fruit jars. This required planning because canning jars were one of the more valuable items on the farm. Farm women kept a close inventory of their jars. Canning season was nearly over by corn-shucking time, so the jars had to be taken during the summer. The women who owned the jars might miss them. We had to watch our fathers carefully to observe them hiding the liquor. We were to sneak to the corn pile with one empty jar and one filled with water. The first jar in the corn pile to be found by the shuckers was not placed too deeply and thus was retrieved relatively easily. When retrieved by us boys, a small portion of whiskey was poured into the empty jar and replaced with water from the other jar. Subsequent jars were a little more difficult. This difficulty led to Bobby getting nervous and taking too much out of the first jar he found. The next day at Mr. Walter Smart's store after Bobby's father's shucking, one of the shuckers was heard to say, "That was some bad liquor in that first jar. That liquor didn't have no kick a'tall."

James was the only one to fail to retrieve liquor. James was the kind of boy who, if he planned to say "shit" on Wednesday, would start turning red on Tuesday and stay red through Thursday. His mother often challenged him for looking sneaky and being either guilty of something bad or planning something with "those boys." His fear of getting caught stopped him from going through with his part.

Eventually we accumulated five pints of liquor. This venture provided a pint to each of us. We stored the liquor down by the swimming hole. There we dug a hole in the bank, wrapped

the jars separately in burlap fertilizer bags, placed them in the hole, and covered them to wait there for "getting drunk day."

Getting-drunk day was planned for a Friday night after corn shucking was over. When getting-drunk day arrived, it was very cold, and our mothers could not understand why we wanted to sleep at the swimming hole. We said that we wanted to camp out one more time before winter. Our mothers sent us off with food and all the bedding we could carry.

When we got to the old swimming hole, we decided not to rush the liquor drinking, so we built a fire and ate first. That was a mistake. The moment came that we had planned so carefully. We stood in a circle, each holding a pint of crystal-clear corn whiskey. Each one of us made a stupid toast. Knowing already that the liquor tasted awful, we screwed the tops off, and in unison turned them up, and took down several huge slugs.

James puked first. I was standing in front of him, and he puked all over me. That started a puke fest by all of us except Hermon. Hermon was walking up and down the riverbank laughing hysterically. He yelled out, "Look here," as he slugged down more liquor.

This was just as the dry heaves started on us. There was nothing left to come up. Bobby had the worst case of dry heaves. Finally, we started to calm down, and Bobby said in a weak, raspy tone, "I think I puked up my asshole."

All that planning and sneaking around had been for naught. A group of puke-covered, sick boys returned home to concerned mothers. Needless to say, we gave up liquor drinking.

Hermon's First Time

Hermon was fifteen years old when he became obsessed with having his first sexual experience with a woman. It became all he could and would talk about. He had no qualms or reservations about how, where, or with whom the deed took place. Just let it happen. His attitude was, "Morality and ethics be damned. I want to get it on." He was older than most of us, and because of his exceptional endowment, he thought that the female world just could not wait for him to launch. For the most part, we younger ones in the Bend lived our lives according to our parents' teachings and the morals taught to us in church—but not so, Hermon.

We tired of Hermon's constant talk about the matter and the continual showing of the "coinpack" condom. He would get violently mad when one of us would say things like, "Ain't that the same one you showed us last year, Hermon?" or "Hermon, ain't that rubber dry rotted?"

Anyway, I told my uncle Hansford Pruitt about Hermon. He suggested something that would take care of him. Uncle Hansford got all us boys together and explained the plan. He told Hermon that he knew a woman who would meet him and have sex with him. I have never seen anyone before or after have the enthusiastic response that Hermon exhibited when told about this opportunity.

The plan was to use an old, abandoned log cabin near the river where we had often camped out. Hermon was told that the woman would meet him there. She would charge five dollars, payable before the act, at the meeting place. Hermon asked no questions except, "When can we do it?"

The arrangements were made for one week hence upon a full moon. Unknown to Hermon, a full moon was important because we wanted to hide and observe the proceedings. Hermon talked about it incessantly for the week leading up to the big event.

It was in the summer, and the momentous occasion was to take place at twelve o'clock midnight because the woman's husband left for work at Dan River Mills usually around eleven o'clock. Hermon was to take bedding that he used to camp out. He was to arrive about an hour before the scheduled time in case the lady got away from her husband a little early. Hermon said over and over, "I will tell y'all all about it."

When the night came, Bobby, James, Sonny, Uncle Hansford, and I took up positions near the old cabin and waited for Hermon to arrive on his father's Ferguson tractor. He was early. I suppose anxiousness got to him—thus the early arrival. We watched him get to the cabin and settle in. Then we waited. At about eleven-thirty we saw an old pickup truck struggling through the rough farm road toward the log cabin. The truck stopped about three hundred feet away.

Suddenly, out of the truck emerged a big man wielding a shotgun. He ran toward the cabin screaming, "So you are the SOB that has been seeing my wife!"

Evidently Hermon was looking out the window. Out through the back door ran Hermon as fast as a gazelle. The man shot in the direction that he was running, but luckily he knew the path well to the river and beyond.

The man started over to where we were. We boys were in full fright mode. Uncle Hansford stood up laughing and said, "I think we pulled a good one on all these boys." The man was a friend of Uncle Hansford's. They sure did pull a prank on us. I understand that the old prank was pulled on quite a few boys, especially in the country. We Bend boys were easily duped because we had never heard of the trick.

I don't know how or when Hermon got his dad's tractor back. We didn't see much of him the remainder of that summer. He never spoke to us about the incident. When asked, he would look sheepish and only say that he would tell us all about it sometime.

I have sometimes wondered how old Hermon was deflowered. I think that it may have been a long time after that experience before he offered his services to a woman again.

Hermon turned sixteen that summer and never returned to school. He got his driver's license and took a job. He was never a part of the old Bend gang again.

Calling Time

Recently I was talking to a young man in his late teens or early twenties. In the course of the conversation, I asked him if he was courting anyone. He had a "deer-in-the-headlights look" that said to me, "He knows nothing of what I speak." I asked him if that term meant anything to him. He replied, "Is it something like suing someone in court?" After a brief continuation in the conversation, we parted with his having no further understanding of the art of courtship, as I know it.

I learned from my fifteen-year-old first cousin once removed Tyler Perkins that it is now called "going out" with a girl. This term applies even if the couple doesn't really go anywhere together, and is applicable to all ages. If they have sex without knowing each other's names, it is called "hooking up." Tyler, claiming he had never hooked up, spoke of "hooking up" as casually as if discussing the purchase of an iPod. Obviously I am woefully ignorant of modern courtship.

In the 1940s and 1950s, boys and girls entering or going through puberty looked forward to courting. This meant that anyone of the opposite sex was fair game. If a boy and girl actually went somewhere together—like a movie or a party—they were said to be dating. If they started to sit together regularly or hang out together at school, they were possibly going steady. They were definitely going steady if the girl started to wear the boy's class ring. If the couple blushed a lot when they met at church or in the hallway at school, it was a clear sign of a mating dance.

Where I grew up in the Bend, no teenagers had cars. This limited mobility made courting somewhat inconvenient. Your hunting was limited to within walking distance for frequent dating or going steady. Your range was broadened if you were willing to date on a farm tractor and even further broadened if you could drive and were given occasional use of the family car. In the early 1950s, tractors were coming into the Bend and were often used for courting transportation. Mules and horses were used before tractors were introduced. You could often see a boy in clean clothes with his hair oiled down with Sur-Lay hair tonic on the farm tractor going over to visit his girlfriend.

If a boy had use of the family car, he would pick up his girlfriend and take her to a movie and a drive-in restaurant for a burger or dog and a milkshake later. There they would run into

many of their friends from school. The talk on the next school day was all about who saw whom and where.

Drive-in restaurants were very popular. A waiter or waitress would come to your car, take your order, and return with your food, without your ever having to leave the car. Our favorite drive-in restaurants were Short Sugar's in Reidsville and the Snack Bar in Mayfield, North Carolina. Rarely did teenagers dine in a sit-down restaurant.

There were also drive-in movie theatres back then. A drive-in was an outdoor theatre with a huge screen. People would sit in their cars with speakers having volume control knobs hanging from their car windows. Drive-in theatres were often called passion pits because of the heavy petting or smooching that went on during the movies. First kisses and an occasional loss of virginity took place at some drive-in picture shows. I went to college with a boy who swore that during high school he had a job at a drive-in theatre knocking on car windows to inform teenage boys and girls that the movie had ended. One of our favorite drive-in theatres was the South Drive-In on Route 29 south of Danville, Virginia.

My girlfriend Lucille Baker and I preferred the sit-in theatres like the Rialto or the North in Danville. Lucille liked movies starring Fred Astaire and Ginger Rogers or westerns featuring Gene Autry or Roy Rogers. Strange as it may sound coming from a Bend boy, I liked romantic movies starring Mario Lanza an Italian operatic tenor and movie star during the 1950s.

I started dating seriously at seventeen. Being raised by a wonderful mother and having three sisters caused me to have great respect for girls. In high school I was considered to be a real gentleman around the ladies. Lucille and I started dating toward the end of the eleventh grade. By age seventeen, my somewhat rowdy days with my Bend buddies had come to an end. I rarely spent time with them anymore. As you will read in the following story, "Breaking Out," I was beginning to develop a more serious view of life.

Limited access to courting transportation resulted in a practice called double-dating. That custom meant that a boy and his buddy would date girls who were friends. Believing it to be safer for their daughters, most parents liked this arrangement. Little did the parents know that smooching could be unashamedly practiced by consenting couples at a drive-in picture show.

Lucille and I mostly double-dated. Sometimes we all four rode in my parents' car, or sometimes we rode in the other boy's family car. On very rare occasions a girl's parents, after gaining trust in their daughter's boyfriend, would allow them the use of the girl's family car. On most Wednesdays I would ride my motorcycle to Lucille's home, and sometimes we would take a breezy ride together in the country.

It wasn't unusual for a boy dating a girl to be disliked by the girl's father. In fact, it was standard practice if a boy was a girl's first suitor.

If a boy walked or rode the farm tractor to court a girl, the date most often meant sitting in the living room in full view of the family. This resulted in a great deal of blushing and awkward conversation, leaving the father to conclude that his daughter was interested in the community idiot.

In the summer a dating couple could garner a bit more privacy by sitting on the front or back porch alone while the family listened to *The Lone Ranger*, *The FBI*, or *The Grand Ole Opry* on the radio. Many a first kiss came out of this environment.

If courting took place in the presence of the family, ridding the family of the boy was easy. The old man could simply say, "Bed time," and the courting came to an immediate and abrupt end.

The call for the young man to leave the premises was more difficult if the courting was occurring on the porch. The lighting of homes was done with oil lamps, and normally there was no light on the porches. Every father had a "calling time" gesture. "Calling time" was a term used to describe a father's signal that it was time for the young man to leave.

Each father had his own gesture for calling time. Some were direct, like, "Young man, it is time to leave." Others were more subtle, like a serious clearing of the throat, cutting off the radio, or dropping heavy work shoes on the floor from an obviously high point. Early in courting, the girl was responsible for identifying the calling time signal. Once learned, however, the boy would dare not challenge the old man.

Lucille did not have a father involved in her life during the time we dated. Mothers evidently did not have calling time privileges. However, Lucille did have a Chihuahua named Prince. Prince would stand in front of us and stare at me as we sat on the couch. He would let out a ferocious growl if I as much as put a hand on Lucille. If I tried to outlast Prince, he would often fall asleep and hit the floor whereupon he would awaken and notify me that he was still on the job. I did not like that dog, but still I was saddened when he died later of cancer.

One night awhile back, I was talking with some friends my age who grew up on farms just as I did. One of the men told us a personal story that I will try to tell here just as he told us. The names are being withheld because the boy married the girl in the story and they live today. You will understand why they would want anonymity when you read the story.

My friend told us that when he was a teenager, he walked over to his girlfriend's home one summer evening. After sitting in the house for awhile and getting I-hate-you looks from her father, he and the girl adjourned to the back porch and left the family playing a card game called Rook. The back porch offered more privacy, and he planned to work up to their first kiss. As it got dark and the right mood was coming on, the girl's old man cleared his throat loudly and dropped his brogan shoes on the floor. The girl jumped up and said, "Time to go." The girl's bedroom window opened onto the back porch, so they agreed that he would leave long enough for her parents to settle down. He was to return and meet her back on the porch after she climbed out onto the porch through her bedroom window.

Everything went according to plan. They were about to have that first kiss and no telling what else. Suddenly they heard her father coming. She scrambled back through her window as he rolled off the porch and snuggled up against the porch foundation wall. It was dark, and the foundation wall of the porch was high enough that he felt perfectly safe. Then the plan went terribly wrong. He said, "As I lay there I could hear the old man clear his throat, yawn, and walk toward my end of the porch. I lay quietly thinking that I was surely going to be caught. A thousand explanations ran through my mind. I knew that her father did not like me, so I was prepared for all hell to come down on me. Instead of hell coming down on me, the old rascal walked to my end of the porch, stretched, yawned, and commenced to pee all over me. I lay there thinking, *I wish he would hold it in one position.* He peed on me from my head to my toes. I don't know if he ever actually looked down to see me, but I have no doubt that he knew that I was there on the ground.

"I left thinking, *I can never come here again. How will I explain to my girlfriend why I am not coming to see her anymore?*

"I laid low for awhile. School was out, so mercifully I didn't have to see her at school. I put the word out that I had been sick.

"Eventually my desire to see my love again overrode my shame, and I dressed in my best clothes and went to see her. When I saw her father, he looked at me in a more welcoming way and even seemed pleased to see me. Naturally I have thought about the incident often. I eventually concluded that the old man decided, 'If that young man can take that treatment and still come around, he may have the right stuff to marry my daughter.' He probably also thought, 'If that action didn't keep him away, I will have to shoot him to get rid of him.'"

My friend said that he was married to his then girlfriend for years before he told her the whole story. Her father became his father-in-law and great friend.

Currently I have a business relationship with my first cousin Angela Perkins and her husband Alex, who live in Danville, and a sibling relationship with my dear sister Elaine who still lives near the Bend where we grew up. These relationships lure me back to Danville and the Bend area frequently. I have had lunch at Short Sugar's a few times; and when I pass the site of the old South Drive-In, I always slow down a bit and let the memories flood by.

Breaking Out

I had a different title for this story until I had a conversation with my friend Rob Tharp, a retired school principal with a respected intellect. We had a wonderful conversation about how a single and seemingly simple act by some interested person can bring about a paradigm shift, a moment when one event can change generations of culture in a person's life. He calls it a "breakout."

This is a breakout story inspired by Rob.

Up until this point, no one in my family's history or anyone from any other family in the Bend had ever attended college. At an early age, I dreamed of getting a college education, making a good salary, seeing some of the world, and feeling comfortable discussing esoteric subjects with educated people. That dream faded as high school graduation came closer and closer. I did have savings that I described in my story, "Turning Twelve." I didn't buy a car like my contemporaries did when I turned sixteen. I opted to ride a small Harley-Davidson motorcycle that I bought for $125.

My thoughts at the time were that the Harley would get me mobile for far less money and leave my savings for college. This strategic plan worked for awhile, but in the summer between the tenth and eleventh grades, I got serious about college costs. It appeared that by the time I needed to enroll in college, I would have enough money to pay college tuition for maybe two years. Then there was room and board to consider. My college fund looked smaller and smaller. At the same time a 1940 Ford coupe at a used-car lot in Danville, Virginia, looked better and better. I was probably the only seventeen-year-old boy without a car. I rode by that used-car lot to look at that '40 Ford coupe until I was, as they say, really in heat for it.

With a '40 Ford coupe, a boy would attract all kind of girls. Like most boys my age, hormones were raging. I was starting to think differently about life—so much so that it scared me—so I decided to put off buying that '40 Ford coupe until after school started. Surely the other guys would be driving cars to school and impressing the girls while I rode the bus or my Harley.

On the first day of eleventh grade, my chemistry teacher Clarence Shipton said to me, "LaVerne, I want to meet with you after class."

I had classes under Mr. Shipton in both the ninth and tenth grades. I really liked and admired him and had done really well in his classes. I stayed after class as he had asked. He looked at me with his dark, penetrating eyes that he used to scare the bejeezus out of misbehaving students and said, "LaVerne, you are going to college to study engineering. In order to get into engineering school, you will need physics. As you know, we don't offer physics here at Ruffin High." He pointed to a large closet behind his desk and said, "I am going to teach you physics in that closet while I am conducting my chemistry class. I have checked your schedule and will see you here for my 10:00 a.m. class tomorrow." With this said, he shoved a physics book at me, turned, and walked away.

I was somewhat in a state of shock; I don't remember saying a word. During my life, events have happened that I recall so vividly that I could stand within a few inches of the spot where I stood when experiencing them and see them again. Lucille and I getting married, President

Kennedy getting assassinated, and watching the second plane fly into the World Trade Center on 9/11 are such vivid events. The day my teacher and mentor Mr. Clarence Shipton had that conversation with me was the most standout moment of my life—that moment that Rob calls a breakout moment. When I got home, I put my savings account book away. I never looked at that '40 Ford coupe again. I appeared before Mr. Shipton the next day at ten; he taught me physics in that closet for two years.

I rode that Harley summer and winter. Somewhat embarrassed because I didn't have a car, I compensated by developing my image as a rebellious type. During the fifties, people who rode motorcycles were considered low class or rebellious in the vein of James Dean of *Rebel without a Cause* movie fame. There was a joke at the time going around: "What is the difference between a Harley rider and a Hoover vacuum cleaner?" The answer was, "Location of the dirt bag." That joke is reflective of people's attitudes toward motorcycle riders during the fifties. I wore a leather motorcycle jacket, high-heeled motorcycle boots, and the standard motorcycle hat. No helmet was required by law back then. My summer hat was in the style of a policeman's cap, black with a white bill. My winter head gear was an aviator's helmet complete with goggles, like Snoopy and the Red Baron wore when flying their Sopwith Camels. I wore my hair in a ducktail. My Harley and I developed quite a reputation. I was the only boy in Ruffin High School who rode a motorcycle.

I learned to love and admire Mr. Shipton so much that I started to adapt his mannerisms. My sisters gave me a Tony Home Permanent so I could style my hair like Mr. Shipton. Mr. Shipton taught me two years of physics and a whole bunch about life. Some kids, in a respectful way, called me "Little Shipton." I didn't know how I was going to do it—attend and complete college, that is—but I was not about to let Mr. Shipton down.

Late in the eleventh grade in Latin class, I sat behind and eventually fell in love with the very pretty, bright, black-haired, brown-eyed Lucille Baker. We started to go steady, as in the fifties we called regularly dating only one person. Daddy would let me use the family car on weekends to date Lucille, and we dated on my motorcycle some. To know Lucille today, you would never believe that refined lady had at one time been a "Harley bitch."

That Harley helped me through college. I attended the Virginia Tech extension school in Danville for the first two years, using my savings to pay for direct college costs. For dorm fees, meals, and books, I used money that I earned working in Bendall's Drug Store four hours every weeknight and eight hours on Saturdays and most Sundays. I rode that Harley to and from work in winter and summer, rain or shine.

Lucille completed a two-year secretarial science course at Danville Technical Institute and was hired to work for the school dean. We got married when we were twenty years old. The

sheriff of Rockingham County sold us a small house trailer that we moved to a Virginia Tech–owned mobile home park in Blacksburg, Virginia. With a recommendation from the dean of Danville Tech, Lucille got a job working for the head of the agricultural engineering department at Virginia Tech and moved to Blacksburg while I stayed back and farmed during the summers between my sophomore and senior years. When Lucille went to work for Danville Tech, she rented a room within walking distance of her job. When she went to Blacksburg ahead of me, we needed transportation so we bought a worn-out 1951 Plymouth for $150. For training purposes, the auto repair students at Danville Tech put that Plymouth into really good condition for us. We drove that car into the ground by the time I graduated. We had quite a struggle, but we made it. When I got my degree, Lucille was invited up on stage and was presented a PHT (Put Hubby Through) certificate. This was an honor Virginia Tech bestowed on wives who helped their husbands through college. Oh, by the way, I could stand in the exact spot where I saw Lucille get that PHT certificate.

I kept up with Mr. Shipton for a few years but eventually lost contact. Around 2001, Lucille and I, along with a former schoolmate, Anne Johnson, met Mr. Shipton in Greensboro for lunch. He was retired at the time from the University of North Carolina at Greensboro. He looked great, even though emphysema caused him to be constantly on oxygen. I visited him regularly for about a year. Mr. Shipton had developed a love for owning and tinkering with sports cars. At the time he owned a little Mazda, but being on oxygen precluded him from driving. Early one morning I was preparing to go to Greensboro to drive him on a trip to the mountains in his Mazda. I was just getting out of the shower when one of his sons called and told me that Mr. Shipton had died peacefully during the night.

Two weeks earlier I had driven him for a regular checkup that resulted in an overnight stay in the hospital. I had taken my 1955 Ruffin High School yearbook with me to show him how I had emulated him in high school. I stayed until he was placed comfortably in a room. Although I had told him before what he had meant to my life, I felt compelled to say more. I told him the '40 Ford and Harley-Davidson story. I told him that my respect for him kept me from ever owning one of the most highly prized cars ever built. I turned to walk away but had to turn back and say once more, "Thank you, sir. I love you for being you, but most of all for the positive influences you have had on my life." I saw a tear in his eye. He smiled and nodded, not saying a word. I relived one of the premier moments of my life as I walked out of that hospital. I couldn't even talk to myself for awhile.

I have often thought about how many people, speaking symbolically, bought that '40 Ford and never had a Clarence Shipton to provide them a breakout moment.

A Boy Named LaVerne?

LaVerne? A boy named Sue? It really doesn't matter if you have to grow up with a girl's name. We all suffer the same humiliating experiences. I never got into a blood, guts, and beer fight with my father as the character did in the song Johnny Cash sang, "A Boy Named Sue." I did have to learn to live with my name. To add to the problem, I grew up with three sisters and no brothers. I'm lucky that I don't squat to pee even today. After years of telemarketers expecting a woman or people expecting a female to show up, I have learned to take advantage of the situation and actually have had fun with my name. For instance, not long ago I received a call from a telemarketer who asked to speak to LaVerne Thornton.

I replied, "I am LaVerne Thornton."

Sounding startled, she exclaimed, "I'm sorry; I was expecting a woman."

I replied, "I am a woman. It's those damn testosterone pills I take so I can get really hot for my husband. They mess up my voice." I asked her, "Honey, do you know what a girl can do about chin hair? What are you calling for, sweetie?" Needless to say, it was an awkward moment for her. She hung up.

The local Jewel Box store in Reidsville, North Carolina, had a custom of giving a small jewelry box made by Lane to all girls upon graduation from high school. Each senior girl received a letter that she was to present to the store when she showed up to get her jewelry box. I got such a letter. Lane was widely known for their cedar hope chests. Most girls in the forties and fifties had a hope chest that they would use for storing household linens and other items in hopes of getting married someday. I went to Reidsville on a Saturday morning with all my manly manners to collect my box. I showed the letter to a woman who worked there.

She looked at me and said, "I'm sorry, but LaVerne Thornton has to come in person to get her box."

I showed her my driver's license and said, "You don't understand, ma'am. I am LaVerne Thornton."

She called the manager over and asked for his decision. The manager saw the humor in the situation and told her to let me have the box. I still have that box, and through the years I have

had a good deal of fun telling the story of how, as far as I know, I am the only male who ever graduated from high school with a girl's "box."

By the way, I bought Lucille's engagement ring and wedding band from the Jewel Box. That experience taught me a little something about sales and the promotion of products.

I have on several occasions gotten on the phone to explain to some wife that I was LaVerne Thornton, the businessperson with whom their husband was having dinner.

I was having pre-op work completed in preparation for prostate surgery a few years ago. One of the most important tests on a male's blood is the PSA or prostate-specific antigen test. Of course, this test is done only on men. This test was particularly important since I was facing prostate surgery. As usual I read all of my test results when they were handed to me. I could not find my PSA reading. After a careful search, I found the reason. "Female" was checked on the patient's sex block. I showed it to the nurse, stood, and motioned to drop my pants to show her that I had all the equipment associated with having a prostate. She assured me that she believed me. Everyone in the office got a chuckle, and the test was repeated. Incidentally, that was the third or fourth time this mistake had been made.

My best "A Boy Named LaVerne" story happened in Portland, Oregon. We had a contract to convert a Calcematic lime kiln from natural gas to coal for a cement company in Portland. No company had ever successfully accomplished this conversion before, so I stayed with the project from start to successful startup. Someone familiar with Portland suggested that I stay in the very old but famous Mallory Hotel. I arrived to claim my reservation late one afternoon on a weekday. The woman checking me in said, "Oh, I saw your reservation and I expected you to be a woman." She continued, "You must be from down South, where they give boys girls' names and give girls boys' names."

"Yes, ma'am. I am from North Carolina but was raised in southern Virginia."

She told me that she was from Alabama and that her name was Billy Jack. Billy Jack asked me if I had ever had trouble with having a girl's name. We exchanged a few stories, like the many times people would be expecting someone of the opposite sex. She really enjoyed the jewelry box story. Billy Jack wasn't busy, so we continued talking, mostly exchanging name stories and southern culture stories. I told her that when I was approaching graduation from high school, I received letters from many of the predominately girls' colleges inviting me to apply to their schools.

Billy Jack laughed and said, "You should have applied."

I told her that I did apply to one girls' school. She asked me what happened. I held my hand up with my thumb and forefinger about two inches apart and replied, "I failed the physical by about this much."

I can't recall seeing someone laugh so hard. I went on to my room. Soon the phone rang. I answered, and it was Billy Jack. She said, "I got so tickled that I forgot to get your signature." I told her that I would be right down to sign and that I was sure relieved that she wasn't coming up to see how badly I failed that physical.

I still run into confusion about having what most people think is a girl's name, but all in all, it has been more fun than aggravation.

Feed-Sack Fashions

"Repair, reuse, make do, and don't throw anything away."

If my mother had been born and lived in different circumstances, she could have easily been a top fashion designer. She could work wonders on an old, Singer, pedal-type sewing machine. She would visit shops in Danville that sold girls' and women's clothes, come home with a few yards of cloth, and without a pattern, make my sisters' school clothes. Today these clothes are called knockoffs. These knockoffs kept my sisters in style. She created her own beautiful fashions for really dressy clothes for my three sisters and herself. Mama and daughters dressed in high fashion on Sundays and special occasions wearing Mama's designs. Dan River Mills had a cotton gingham plant in Danville. Gingham was made by weaving colored threads together to create a pattern. Dan River Mills had a company store where employees could purchase gingham at discount prices. Mama would often buy gingham through a relative who worked in the mill. Although the prices were discounted, it was still expensive for farm folks, so gingham was only bought for especially dressy Sunday clothes. Most of my mama's and sisters' everyday clothes were made of less expensive print fabric. The pattern on print fabric is, as the name implies, printed onto the cotton. The pattern on print would fade faster than gingham as it was laundered. As the school year progressed, you could see the pattern gradually fade away. As my sisters reached their teen years, wearing faded print dresses became a source of embarrassment for them and a source of pain for my mother. Mama would love to have been able to provide fancier things for her girls. However faded their print dresses, my sisters always went out clean and starched.

Everyone in the Bend raised hogs. We grew them big and fat. When neighbors got together at hog-killing time, the farmer with the fattest hogs got bragging rights. My father usually traded honors with our neighbor on the next farm, Emit Hazelwood, for having the heaviest and fattest hogs. We raised three hogs every year that averaged six hundred pounds each. These fat hogs yielded more than enough cooking lard to last until hog-killing time came around again. My dad cured the best country ham on earth. Six hams weighing about forty-five pounds

each were more than our family needed, so Daddy traded country hams with Dr. Dillard and our dentist Dr. Snead for our family's medical and dental needs.

You may ask what fat hogs have to do with print dresses? Well, raising fat, high-lard-yielding hogs requires a large amount of food. We fed those hogs every edible scrap available, including garden stuff that may have otherwise gone to waste. To balance out their diet, we fed them a store-bought supplement that came in bags made of cotton and were normally white with a picture of a sailing ship on them; I don't remember the name of it or what it contained. We called it "ship stuff." Mama used those bags to make pajamas for me and night dresses for the girls. I remember a pair of pajamas she made for me that she cut just right so that the ship picture was perfectly centered on the back of the top. You could say it was the first shirt with a company logo on it, an original. They were a forties' version of Abercrombie & Fitch designer pajamas.

Occasionally the ship stuff came in beautiful, colorful print cotton bags. The primary purpose for these colorful print bags was to attract buyers to their product by enticing the women and girls to get the men to buy the ship stuff that came in those bags, which could be used to make beautiful feed-sack dresses. If you visited Mr. Walter Smart's store on the day that the feed truck came, you would see farm women and girls climbing over and through the bags looking for just the right bags to make dresses.

I heard Mr. Smart tell Daddy one time that a fat mama and her two daughters were going through the feed bags, and he overheard the little girl shout, "This one is mine!"

Her older sister replied, "No, it is not. You stay away from that one; there are two bags with the same pattern, and that is enough for Mama to make herself a dress."

We kept the food scraps in a five-gallon slop bucket. Twice a day my older sister Betty Jean and I would take the bucket down to the pigpen and slop the hogs. We were too little to carry a full bucket alone, so Daddy made a carrying stick that we would place under the bucket bell (handle). I took one side and she took the other. We stirred in a measured amount of ship stuff, carried it to the pigpen, and poured it into the feeding trough. The worst spankings my sister and I ever got came the time we stood with the slop bucket full of food about fifty feet from the trough, laughing hysterically while the hogs went into a squealing frenzy. Daddy told us that if he ever caught us torturing any farm animal again, the punishment would be worse.

As I told you in my breaking-out story, Lucille and I got married when we were twenty years old. I was approaching my third year at Virginia Tech. She got a job there working for a professor in the agricultural engineering department. We lived in a trailer thirty feet long and eight feet wide on a lot owned by the university. Lucille sacrificed a great deal to help me through college. She had little more to wear than five print dresses made by my mother. I remember one time, a day before Lucille got paid, we had only one can of Campbell's soup left

for our day's food. I recall watching her leave for work that morning wearing a print dress that Mama had made. The skirt had small brown, green, and yellow flowers. The top was solid dark brown and had a boy collar that was made from the same material as the skirt. Lucille grew prettier as she grew older, but she has never been more beautiful than on that one-can-of-soup day, when she left for work wearing that print dress that Mama made. I was so very proud of Lucille when she walked up on stage at my graduation from Virginia Tech to receive her PHT (Put Hubby Through) certificate.

Lye Soap

I loved my mother. I would do anything she asked me to do, and I would do it 'til she told me to stop. If she were to ask me to dig a hole, I would dig until she said stop. If she went away and forgot that I was digging a hole, I might wind up in China. Such was the case once when we were making lye soap.

Most people these days have never heard of lye soap. To make it, you save the ashes from the wood you heated your house with in the winter. Oak is preferred. When preparing to make lye soap, which is always done in very cold weather, you put the ashes in a container and cover them with water. After this mixture has soaked for awhile, the water becomes very alkaline. The mixture is then strained and saved to mix with hog fat to make lye soap. All country folks raised hogs from which we would make lard, a staple of the southern diet. We all had a large, black iron pot mounted on bricks or rocks in our backyards. If you went by someone's home and didn't see a black iron pot in the backyard, you would assume that they had moved. I went home with a schoolmate and stayed overnight one time. After coming home, I told my mama, "Jimmy's folks are the poorest people I have ever seen; they don't even have a black iron pot." This pot was used to boil clothes, to render hog fat into lard, and to make lye soap.

To make lye soap you put about an equal amount of the alkaline water and hog fat into the black iron pot. Then a fire is built under the pot, and the mixture is constantly stirred while it boils. The trick is to stir the boiling mixture until the stirring stick will stand upright in the mix. The mix is then dipped and smoothed into flat pans to a thickness of about two inches. It is cut into bars of soap after it hardens, which can take about a month.

One time I was assigned by my mama to stir the lye soap. It was about two degrees that day with a fierce wind. I had so many clothes on that stirring was a chore. Mama told me to stir the pot until she got back to check on me. I stirred and I stirred, and Mama didn't come back. But Mama said "stir," so I stirred. I stood and stirred in that cold wind until I had six-inch snotsicles hanging from each nostril, and the toes of my shoes burned off from having to stand so close to the fire to stir. My only thought was that Mama was going to kill me for burning the toes off my shoes. The philosophy back then was, "You can grow new toes back,

but shoes cost a lot of money." When Mama finally got back, she took me inside, cried, and lovingly hugged me for a long time. That soap turned out perfectly, or at least as perfectly as lye soap can be.

Something developed between Mama and me that day, a kind of bonding that lasted until her death at eighty-six in 1997.

The love sure came in handy, because I was always guilty of something punishable by Mama. A long time went by before I was scolded for anything I did. I rode it to the limit. That was the only time while I was growing up that I got two pairs of shoes in one year. Just Mama and I went to Efirds' Department Store basement in Danville and bought new Buster Brown shoes for me. Because of World War II rationing, there was a certain method to buying shoes back then. You would put a hard rubber spacer in the toe of the Buster Brown shoes that were larger than your size. This provided for growing room. You would wear the shoes with the spacers until you walked sort of clubfooted. Then you took the spacers out and walked with your shoes flapping the floor until your feet grew some or you learned to walk with loose shoes. At school you would hear someone say, "Kelly has grown some 'cause his shoes are flapping the floor."

All of us country kids smelled of lye soap. Our clothes were washed in it; we bathed in it and cleaned our house with it. I said a bad word once, and Mama washed my mouth out with lye soap. I was thirty-seven years old before I said "shit" again. It only takes one lye-soap mouth washing to provoke repentance from a kid. I really believe that you could have a kid memorize the Ten Commandments, wash his mouth out with lye soap, and say, "If you ever break one of these commandments, I am going to wash your mouth out with lye soap again." You would raise a Ten Commandment-perfect kid. Our son Perry once said "damn" at what I thought was a perfectly appropriate time to say "damn." Lucille disagreed and washed his mouth out with Ivory soap. My thought was, *How can a kid learn a lesson by having his mouth washed out with store-bought soap?* Law enforcement has overlooked lye-soap mouth washing as an effective lie-detector, crime-prevention tool. Just think of the potential for the use of lye-soap mouth washing in the war on terror. Take one terrorist, wash his mouth out with lye soap, and the next one in line would either beg for pig blood or scream, "I know where bin Laden is!"

I used to visit my cousin Larry in Danville. One of these visits would be in the spring when we country kids got out of school early to work in the fields. City schools were still in session. On one such visit I went to Larry's school with him. I was welcomed by the teacher and his classmates. I was given a chair and was allowed to sit by Larry. He sat behind a pretty girl who smelled so sweet. It was the first time that I had smelled a girl up close, not smelling of lye soap. I got a tingle in my growing area.

Years after rationing was cancelled and we all used sweet-smelling store-bought soap, my youthful memories faded until I was reminded again of my lye-soap experiences. I was in a quaint little soap and candle shop and caught the faint and familiar scent of lye soap. I followed that smell and found the source—a big box of old-fashioned lye soap. I bought a chunk and carried it in my briefcase wrapped in a plastic wrapper to preserve its full-strength odor. I would amuse my business associates by occasionally taking it out and asking them to identify it. No one ever guessed right. Some called it rotten fish carcass. Some called it crystallized skunk fart.

For years when I got "too big for my britches," as Mama would often accuse me, I would take out that lye soap, smell it, and take myself back to my humble upbringing.

I think I will see if I can find another chunk of lye soap. Maybe Google knows where to find some. Perhaps you would like to find and experience a bar or two of lye soap yourself.

Wash Day

I just came back from the laundry where I picked up four pairs of pants and six shirts. I hung the clean, pressed pants and the clean, starched, and ironed shirts in my closet alongside many other shirts and pants. I stood there momentarily and thought, *Four pairs of pants and six shirts is a larger wardrobe of shirts and pants than I ever had at any one time growing up.* The only work I had to do to keep them clean was to drive to the laundry. Having grown up in the forties and fifties, I still find it difficult to imagine the work involved in doing laundry back then. Wash day on the farm had many work-intensive portions.

If we were lucky, our rain barrels would be full on wash day. Every farmhouse in the Bend had a metal (tin) roof. Rain gutters were not installed to take the water away from the house but were put there to collect rainwater for washing clothes.

Also, Mama and my sisters swore by rainwater for washing their hair. If the rain barrels had not collected enough water for wash day, the water was brought up from the spring to either fill or top off the barrels. In the summertime it was rare to have full barrels on wash day. The barrels held fifty-five gallons. It took about one of those barrels for a washing. Filling the barrels was the children's chore. Any of us kids who were strong enough to carry a gallon bucket full of water joined in. I remember being very proud to join my older sister Betty Jean in helping to fill the barrels. I was also very proud as I grew strong enough to move up a bucket size. I would have missed the joy of contributing to my family's welfare, let alone the wonderful exercise. By the time all four of us kids were involved in carrying water, it took us five trips each per barrel. We measured most chores on the farm in time. One of my first jobs in management was in manufacturing. Having to manufacture things in a sequence of timed events came naturally to me. I learned it on the farm. I have had people working for me through the years who studied those concepts in college but still never understood the principles thoroughly.

On the mornings of wash day we were up early. Before breakfast one of us was assigned to transfer water from the rain barrel to the black iron pot mounted in the backyard. While the pot was being filled about one-half full, leaving room to add the soiled clothes, a fire was being built under the pot. The wood was cut from trees on the farm into about six-foot logs and dried

through the winter. The logs were then cut into two-foot lengths and further split into several smaller pieces to be used as fuel for the wood cookstove and for fires under the iron pot. The same pot was used for making lye soap, Brunswick stew, and lard. More water was transferred from the rain barrel to two rinse-water tubs sitting on the back porch away from the wash pot.

The next step was to scrape or shave a bar of homemade lye soap, made as described in my previous "Lye Soap" story, into the wash pot. While the water was coming to a boil, we went inside for breakfast. After breakfast, when school was in session, the remainder of the clothes washing was left for Mama. If we weren't in school, all of us kids chipped in unless fieldwork was required, whereupon we went to the fields to work.

Whether Mama worked alone or we assisted her, there was plenty more to do on wash day. The soiled clothes were separated into three piles: coloreds, whites, and rough items, such as work clothes, dishrags, drying cloths, cleaning rags, and so on. Spots on the whites were dipped in the hot water, soaped, and then scrubbed on the washboard to remove spots.

They were placed in the boiling water for awhile, removed with an old broomstick, rinsed once in one tub, and then rinsed in another tub. Next, they were wrung out on the wringer and laid aside for starching and hanging on the clothesline later. While the whites were being rinsed and wrung, the coloreds were put in the wash pot to boil awhile. Then they were rinsed, wrung, and hung on the clothesline after it had been cleaned and dried with a cleaning rag that was then put into the final rough-items load in the old, black iron pot.

Somewhere in this sequence, a tired Mama made starch by putting a measured amount of flour in cool water, smoothing it down, and thinning it with boiling water. The clothes that were to be starched were dipped in the starch mixture, wrung again, and hung on the clothesline. On wash day Mama wore an apron with huge pockets, which were loaded with clothespins.

Mama took a basket of the whites to the clothesline and pinned them to the line by the tails so as not to leave marks on the parts of the garments that were visible when worn. All of this work was often done with a crying toddler tugging at her dress or coattails. In the winter the clothes sometimes froze on the line and took extremely long to dry. The coloreds were then hung. Last, the rough items were hung over the line or draped over shrubs and bushes to dry. Ultimately, the wash water was used in the summer to water the flower beds and garden. The still warm soapy water from the iron pot was used to scrub the back porch. An exhausted Mama finished the wash day in time to prepare a hot meal on a wood cookstove for Daddy and us kids returning from farm chores. Mama took little comfort in knowing that ironing was awaiting her the next morning.

In 1948 Mama got a gasoline-powered washing machine. I remember the look of excitement on her face when she kick-started that Briggs and Stratton motor. The water still had to be heated in the old pot but the washboard was thrown aside, waiting to be used for another unknown purpose.

There was a little more to wash day and laundry cleaning in the forties than just driving to MacDuff's Cleaners in Sanford, North Carolina, or to your local Laundromat or dry cleaners, wouldn't you say? I seriously wonder how any farm couple found time or had the energy to procreate.

Whitewash

I was listening to a news analysis program on XM radio recently. The segment at the time was about a charge of improper behavior by employees in the U.S. Justice Department. The Justice Department announced that it was conducting an internal investigation on the matter. One of the pundits used one of my favorite expressions to describe the situation. He said, "It would be like hiring Dracula to guard the blood bank." Another pundit allowed as how conducting an internal investigation would be a "whitewash." Certainly we all understand what a whitewashing is in such circumstances.

I was anxious to arrive at the walking trail where I have been walking with my friend Dave Watson for nineteen years. We always have a number of subjects to talk about as we walk. As we started out, I asked Dave, "What is the first thought you have when I say the word 'whitewash'?" I was expecting him to say that it probably would be describing a cover-up.

His answer surprised me. Dave said, "When I was a kid in Georgia, the folks whitewashed the bottoms of pecan trees. I think it was to prevent sun damage and to control certain insects." I was really delighted at his answer because Dave pointed out a meaning of the word that I had not considered. He asked me what "whitewash" meant to me.

I explained to him that since I have been writing stories about growing up in the Bend, a great number of things happen that remind me of how different life is today from when I grew up. For instance, the word "whitewash" brought back memories of log cabins that dotted the forest and farms in the Bend. The early settlers in the Bend built two-story homes with logs cut from local trees. The family kitchen and living quarters were on the first floor. The parents usually slept on the first floor, and all the kids slept upstairs. As time went on and the family could afford it, shed rooms were built onto the back of houses. A shed room would become the kitchen, and a wood-burning cookstove would be added. The most commonly used trees selected for building these log cabins were white oaks and red oaks. The logs were cut to whatever wall length could be achieved. They were roughly hand-hewn into square shapes and notched on the ends so that when laid one on top of the other, the logs would come close to touching along the length. When manufactured roofing was not available, cedar shingles were

hand-hewn from local cedar trees. The Bend had a prolific array of small metamorphic rocks that could be gathered and used to build the chimneys. All the chimneys on log houses in the Bend were built from those rocks. A family settling in the Bend could, with a crosscut saw and an axe, build their home with their own hands out of local materials. The fireplaces served as heating systems in winter and cooking places year-round. Most of the fireplaces eventually added swinging metal hooks from which you could hang pots for cooking. These cabins would be cozy and warm in the winter but could be really hot in the summer when the fireplace was being used to cook the family meal.

I had a black childhood buddy named Jimmy who lived in a log cabin. I have really fond memories of popping popcorn in his family's fireplace on cold winter nights. Incidentally, it was popcorn that we raised ourselves. The popper was a wire basket with a long handle. We put the popcorn in the basket, held it over the fireplace flame, and shook it briskly until the corn popped. We buttered it with homemade cow's butter, added salt, and had a delicious treat. To make popcorn balls, my mother would sometimes roll popcorn in homemade molasses or wild honey that we got from a hive in the woods. To really jack up the flavor, butter was added to the honey. After they hardened a bit, you had a great snack.

So where does whitewash play a part in these log cabin stories? There are wide spaces between the logs. These gaps or chinks were partially filled with chink wood. Chink wood is the short sections of the same oak tree split into wedge-shaped pieces. These wedges were hand-shaped, flattened on the wide side, and fitted into the spaces or chinks in the walls. The goal was to hand chisel and plane these pieces to fit snugly into the chinks in the interior walls to make the walls as flat and smooth as possible. The same thing was done to the exterior walls but with less emphasis on detail. The next step was to make a mixture of red clay and water mixed to the same consistency as today's brick mortar. The clay mixture called daubing was applied to the interior walls much as you would apply plaster. This process was repeated, applying several thin layers at a time. Time for thorough drying was allowed between applications. The finished product was a smooth red wall, relatively crack-free. The exterior walls were similarly treated again with less attention to detail. To really class up the place a family would whitewash the walls. Several whitewash pits were located in the Bend. These pits were deposits of pure, white, fine, textured clay.

Looking back, it was probably kaolin clay. My grandmother Essie's farm had a whitewash pit where most people in the Bend got their clay. Most families whitewashed their walls in the spring. Whitewashing day was a family affair. The furnishings were moved outside, and the entire family pitched in to brush on the whitewash. The results were crisp, clean, pure, white walls that would be the envy of any interior designer. An added bonus was the smell in

the house after whitewashing, which was similar to the fresh scent of the air after a summer thunderstorm.

These whitewash pits served another purpose. Some southern blacks and poor whites had a custom of eating clay. My grandmother's whitewash pit was visited by people from areas far outside the Bend. The deposit there was especially large and exceptionally white.

The practice of eating dirt, usually fine clays, is so common in so many societies that it must be regarded as a normal human behavior rather than an oddity, according to scientists who are studying it. Yet why hundreds of millions of people and dozens of animal species consume earth remains a mystery, and information about the health effects is contradictory and incomplete.

Some evidence indicates that consumption of soils, a practice known as geophagy, can supply minerals otherwise deficient in local diets; fight nausea, indigestion, and diarrhea; and even counter ingested poisons.

Upon a return visit, some black folks who had migrated north would ask my grandmother for permission to get some clay to take back home. The black folks living in the Bend would often send clay to relatives who had moved away. It seems quaint to me now, but seeing people visiting my grandmother's pit to get clay for whitewashing walls or to get clay for medicinal purposes seemed perfectly normal activities to me back then.

Several families lived in log cabins while I was growing up. Eventually, as the young people left for better economic opportunities as did I, and the older people died, these cabins were abandoned and rotted away. I acquired two farms in the Bend. One had a log cabin on it which were really two structures placed about twelve feet apart with an enclosed breezeway connecting them. A shed room was built across the back of one. It was the last lived-in log cabin in the Bend and was in bad condition when I bought it from relatives. There were six families scattered to various places who owned the farm. Some of them grew up in that old cabin; one family had relocated to England.

My father possessed all the old skills needed to restore that cabin. The last day that my dad and I spent together was at the old cabin. We had agreed that he would stop farming and I would pay him to restore the log cabin. My wife Lucille and I, along with our children LaVisa and Perry, stayed overnight with Mama and Daddy that Saturday. When we left on Sunday, my dad was really excited about our plans for the old cabin. One of the last things my dad said that Saturday was, "I don't think it is possible to duplicate the taste of fried chicken and banana pudding cooked in a fireplace in a log cabin."

I replied, "What about possum?"

Dad grinned and said, "I can live out my time without having possum again." We agreed that upon completion of the restoration, we would fry chicken and make banana pudding as a dedication and celebration meal.

The next day, Monday, Dad suffered an aneurysm. He died a week later. Two painful losses happened on that Monday. I lost interest in things for a long while. By the time my interest was renewed, I could not find anyone qualified to restore that old cabin. Eventually, the farms became a bit of a nuisance and I sold them. If I had starting writing these stories before I sold the farms, I would still have them today.

Waste Not

I took our roll-out trash container to the curb this morning for pick-up by Waste Management garbage service. Waste Management—now that is some name for a company. The company name was based on the fact that we produce so much waste in this country that we have created a gigantic trash management problem. I hate to take out the trash. It's not because I'm lazy or slovenly. I have come to the conclusion that it is rooted in my childhood experiences. We didn't have trash—oh, maybe a smidgen occasionally like a medicine bottle, a broken canning jar, or some such item, for which absolutely no further use could be found. Broken metal parts and worn-out farm implement parts such as plow points were scattered all over the farm or kept in a separate pile for sale to the scrap metal man.

My refuse container had more stuff in it than my family would accumulate in a year on the farm. Our parents taught us to consider carefully every possible use for something before we threw it away. Quite a few items in the container that I took out this morning could have been used for something on the farm.

All families had their own landfill that was located in a wooded area way off in the backyard. We didn't have plastics so most everything that we discarded, except glass, would decay or rust away. The pile grew so slowly that it remained about the same size for years.

Just about everything left over from things we bought was used for something. For instance, we bought Pilot Knob coffee because it came in gallon buckets. We used those buckets for many chores on the farm. They were the starter buckets for the smaller kids when they started bringing water up from the spring and when they started to bring water to fill the tobacco planters.

When we were lucky enough to buy a soft drink, we would usually get RC Cola because you would get just about twice as much RC as you did Coca-Cola for the same money. Daddy taught us to take the top carefully off the cola so as to maintain the integrity of the cap and cork seal. This was done by lifting the cap a little at a time all the way around the bottle, gently removing the cap. The bottle could be filled with homemade tomato juice, and the cap could be placed back on the bottle using a gentle tap with a rubber hammer.

One-gallon glass vinegar jugs were used to keep buttermilk cool in a milk cooling box that was installed in our spring branch. These bottles were designed to allow water to flow through and over the buttermilk to keep it cool.

Any and all table scraps were collected in slop buckets and fed to the hogs.

The newspapers and the *Progressive Farmer* magazines were saved and used to start fires in the wood cookstove year round and in wood heaters in the winter. They were also used for cleaning. One of the first chores we children were assigned was cleaning oil lamp globes. Oil lamps would collect smut on the inside and had to be cleaned. Small hands were just the thing to clean the globes. A wad of newspaper in a child's hand could be fitted through the bottom of the globe, and with a little training the child could wipe clean the interior of the globe. Even today some people use newspapers to clean windows and mirrors.

While a small child was cleaning the globe, an older one would trim off the charred section of the wick and refill the lamp with kerosene, or as we called it, lamp oil. Sometimes we got in trouble smutting each other's faces. This was tolerated by our parents to a point, but as usual, children's play can get out of hand and we would get each other's clothes dirty with smut or, God forbid, we would break a lamp globe. Smutty clothes were usually overlooked. Broken lamp globes were a different matter. Lamp globes cost a good deal of money; breaking one resulted in extra chores for the one at fault.

Some medicine bottles were thrown in the outhouse holes. Whiskey drinkers have been known to discard empty liquor bottles in the outhouse holes to hide the evidence. Who is going to stick his head into an outhouse seat to see what is down there? A cottage industry sprung up among bottle collectors some time ago. Collectors would dig in the outhouse holes of old homesteads in search of rare bottles.

My Bend buddies and I planned to turn Mr. Gaulden over in his outhouse. We never pulled it off. It is the only act of devilment that we ever chickened out on. We didn't chicken out from concern for Mr. Gaulden or for shame. We could not figure out an escape route that would prevent us from being seen upon our retreat. His outhouse sat in a wide-open area, and someone was always around who could see us coming and going. Also, the word in the Bend was that Mr. Gaulden was handy with a gun and a knife.

As far back as I can remember, I heard war talk. I was born on February 17, 1937. World War II officially started on September 1, 1939, when Germany invaded Poland. I was two and one-half years old. The Japanese bombed Pearl Harbor on December 7, 1941, when I was almost five. There were so many subjects that adults of that era would not discuss in the presence of children, such as cancer, pregnancy, and most serious illnesses. War, the most hurtful subject to my ears, was discussed freely. Listening to my granny, Shotgun Essie, read the paper to Aunt Jenny and talk

about my uncles and Aunt Jenny's son being at war conjured up some horrible images in my mind. I always had a vivid imagination, and it went wild listening to them. After growing up and learning the facts about war, my imagination and memories of World War II were not overly vivid at all. What really went on was beyond anything my child's mind could conjure up.

What does war have to do with waste?

As I already mentioned, we saved most scrap metal in a separate pile in hopes of someday selling it for scrap. The Great Depression and Hoover Days, as most folks called the era from which we were just emerging, had eliminated the market for scrap. However, the war effort brought on a huge demand for scrap metal. Metal was required to manufacture all types of war materials, from guns to tanks to planes and more. Kids everywhere got in on the act of supplying scrap metal. I didn't have that famous little red American Flyer wagon that was popular back then, but Daddy had made us a homemade snow sled. My older sister and I dragged that sled around the farm, winter and summer, gathering up every piece of metal we could find. We scoured every field, pasture, and meadow looking for metal. Betty Jean, Elaine, Brenda, and I would team up to pull the scrap, steel-laden sled to the side of Gravel Hill Road and leave it for the scrap man. I don't think that we got or expected money for the metal. We only wanted to help defeat the Germans and Japanese with whom we were at war. I remember looking into the sky when a plane flew over and wondering if it was made from our scrap metal. We looked at pictures of warships in the *Danville Register* newspaper and wondered if they were made with some of our scrap metal. You might say that at six, seven, eight, and nine years of age, I had an up-close and personal relationship with World War II. I believed then and I believe now that I and kids like me helped win that war. Underlying this is a belief that the term that I grew up with, "waste not," also helped win World War II.

As a result of our practice of finding a use for everything, the Bend was a litter-free neighborhood.

I have seen only one other litter-free area in the world since I left the Bend. Cuba was free of litter for the same reason that the Bend was; extremely poor people, who can't afford to waste "good waste," live there.

In 1985, Lucille and I, along with our friends Tommy and Shirley Peyton, were on North Caicos in the Turks and Caicos Islands. We chartered a British registered plane and flew to Santiago, Cuba. It was illegal for Americans to travel to Cuba then, but my experiences growing up in the Bend taught me that you miss a bunch of great experiences in life by follow- ing rules all the time. Those people were in dire poverty. I could write on and on about those experiences. I will say this: Santiago was the cleanest, most litter-free place that we have ever seen. It is simply because people that poor have very little that generates waste. Even a gum wrapper can be used to stop a small leak in a tin-roofed shack for awhile.

Well, I have just finished drinking Diet Cheerwine from a plastic bottle. I could save the bottle to store homemade tomato juice as we did with RC Cola bottles in the forties. I could punch small holes in the cap and use it to sprinkle starch water on the clothes that need ironing. I could get some friends together and play spin the bottle. I will, however, throw it into the already half-filled Waste Management roll-out container to join all the other useful stuff in the landfill.

Southern Revivals

A popular practice in southern churches was the revival. Revivals were particularly important in rural neighborhoods where the church was the center of social activity. These events were generally conducted in July or August, depending to a degree on the long-range weather forecast. Choosing the hottest days for the revivals based upon the forecasted temperatures seemed to be the primary objective. Rural southern ministers loved to see people suffer. There is probably more in the Bible about suffering than any other subject. We are charged to suffer with joy. Suffering strengthens and clarifies our character, so holding a southern revival in July or August, before the advent of air-conditioning, seemed perfect. The minister could hope for someone to suffer from heat stroke during the service, thus adding a touch of drama to the program and allowing the minister to proclaim that this poor soul has been overcome by the spirit of the Lord.

I remember a day two summers ago when a man ran a red light and T-boned my truck. My truck and I spun 365 degrees, rolled completely over, and back upright. People looked at me as if the wreck had made me crazy when I crawled out of the wreck screaming, "Thank you, Jesus! Thank you, Jesus!" You see, under the daze brought on by the wreck, my memories of southern revivals came back, and I gave praise for my chance to suffer and to be saved.

Preachers loved having revival for two primary reasons: they gave sinners and backsliders several opportunities to renew their commitments to the Lord, and they gave preachers ideal forums to recruit new converts. For us kids, revivals gave us good chances to see who in the congregation had sinned. The preacher was usually a visiting minister who could preach real hellfire-and-brimstone sermons. At the conclusion of the sermon there would always be an altar call. The preacher would announce the hymn, usually something like "Just As I Am." While the hymn was being sung, he would invite people to come to the altar for prayer. If no one came forward after singing the verses over and over, maybe twenty-seven times, the preacher would ask for every head to be bowed and every eye to be closed. Then he would plead with people to raise their hands, while no one but God was watching, and confess that they had sinned and needed to be saved. I ask you, could you resist peeping? I had a way of cupping

my hands over my eyes with enough space between my fingers to provide peep room. The next week was filled with gossip about what kinds of sin were committed by the hand raisers. If anyone dared go to the altar, they were the talk of the neighborhood. Someone always went up, or the service would never end. We would count on the same people to go up every year. I often thought that some people went up just to bring the service to an end. One night the minister did a sermon on sinful fornication. I didn't know what fornication was, but I was tempted to run to the altar screaming, "I fornicated! I fornicated!" in an attempt to bring that miserably hot evening to a close.

These services took place while the congregation was packed together waving funeral home fans. You have to be quite old to know about funeral home fans. These fans were made by stapling an eight-inch square piece of cardboard to a piece of wood resembling a tongue depressor about twelve inches long. They would usually have a Bible scene on one side and an ad for the funeral home on the other side. The fan was held in the hand and waved back and forth in front of the face in a feeble attempt to avoid heat exhaustion. Funeral homes provided these fans for free and received free advertising in exchange. We had a bunch of fat ladies who smelled of lye soap and loved those funeral home fans. Unfortunately, these fans did little more than blend body odors and move them around.

I had one suit, a wool knickers suit. A knickers suit has pants like golfers used to wear. The pants have a stretchy band that fits snugly around the calves of your legs. They slide down; you jerk them up. They slide down; you jerk them up. This action takes all your skin off after one hour of wearing a wool knickers suit. One sermon that a revival minister preached was about all those heathens who don't attend church. I'm thinking, *Don't attend church; wonder if heathen kids have to wear wool knickers suits?* If not, it could make a kid want to become a heathen. If Moses had ever worn a wool knickers suit to a southern revival in July, there would be eleven commandments and a modification to the one about murder. The eleventh commandment would be, "Thou shalt not maketh a kid wear a wool knickers suit to a southern revival in July." The "Thou shalt not kill" commandment would read, "Thou shalt not kill unless someone maketh thee wear a wool knickers suit to a southern revival in July."

The revival would last for six days and wind up with all-day preaching and dinner on the grounds on Sunday. Gol-lee, yip-ee! All-day preaching and dinner on the grounds; that's what I'm talking about!

Before air-conditioning and fellowship halls, each rural church had a long picnic table built out under the trees. The table provided a place to put the covered dishes brought to the "dinner on the grounds" event. Women could be heard pointing out what they brought to the dinner and urging everyone they could corner to try their dishes. When the time came to bring the food to the table, my dad would say, "LaVerne, carry the box to the table and carry it like it is mighty heavy."

The picnic table was built about chest high to the average adult, which prevented small children from having any idea what foods were on the table. These kids were stuck with whatever their parents would put on their plates. At one dinner on the grounds, a neighbor's kid about four years old figured out some way to climb unnoticed onto the table. When first seen, he was standing with one foot in a bowl of deviled eggs.

The afternoons would be filled with singing. The singers were usually a male quartet and a woman pianist. The men usually had shiny false teeth, matching colorful jackets, matching pants, and cheap-looking toupees. The piano player was usually a fat lady with a huge Ann Landers hairdo.

Now, across the street and about one-tenth of a mile up the road was the all-black Blue Stone Baptist Church. These people really knew how to have an all-day preaching and dinner-on-the-grounds affair. Once a year they would have a "So-sation (Association) Meeting." When these meetings occurred, about five of us kids would tell our mothers that we were going home with each other. What we really did was slip deep into the woods behind the Blue Stone Baptist Church and watch the "so-sation" proceedings while hidden in thick forest growth. Attendees would set up concessions in the woods and conduct activities such as selling or giving away religious literature, selling drinks and snacks, and generally conducting little kiosk business activities. Way back in the woods liquor was sold. Occasionally, a fight would break out. It made for an exciting and entertaining afternoon. We would go home with all these exciting things to tell but with no possibility of telling our parents.

At one revival meeting, a teenager named Sally, who was a little bit on "the wild side" as we said back then, "got saved." After the service, Hermon, with a very serious look on his face, whispered to us boys, "Do you reckon Sally gonna stop puttin' out?"

The Poorhouse

"I brought you into this world, and I can take you out!"

"Would you look at that dirt on the back of your neck?"

"You have cut yourself and have gotten blood all over your new overalls."

We have all heard what I call "momisms." When I was a kid, I imagined that when a woman got in "the family way" for the first time, she went to a special class to learn momisms. It took me until we were raising our own kids to find out the facts.

I had long forgotten momisms until I came home one day and heard Lucille's voice coming from inside the house saying, "If I told you once, I told you a million times." These things are in a woman's genes along with the ability to see from the back of her head and to detect a kid lying better than a modern-day lie detector. Genes allow a woman to clean rust off chrome with spit on a tissue and give her the skill to untangle a kid's pee-soaked shoestring knot with her teeth.

I recently heard two women talking. One of them said, "I am beginning to sound just like my mother." No little lady, it's in your genes.

My mother's most often used momisms were the "raised in a barn" comment and "Stop that or we are going to wind up in the poorhouse."

My mother shouted, "Were you raised in a barn?" at me one day, and I started thinking, *The room I sleep in is just as cold as it is on the outside. I sleep under twelve homemade patchwork quilts. That makes it pretty close to being raised in a barn.* I aimed to answer her "Yes" someday, but love for her and awesome fear of making her mad always stopped me. Incidentally, I was in an antique shop once and saw some old handmade quilts like I grew up sleeping under. I looked at the prices and reckoned that twelve of those quilts would be worth as much today as the house I grew up in plus the land it sat on.

I heard, "Stop that or you are going to put us in the poorhouse," really often. I never really understood that momism since I thought that we pretty much were already in the poorhouse. This thought vanished from my mind the first time I went into a real "poorhouse." When I was twelve, I joined the Methodist Youth Fellowship at Hickory Grove Methodist Church. This was a beautiful church built of round stones which contained quartz crystals that looked like real, giant diamonds. Most of the stones came from ancestral land on my mother's side of the family.

One of the annual activities for the MYF was to sing for the people at the county poorhouse. In the forties there were no social programs of any kind. Politicians had not yet learned how, in order to ensure their reelection, to create social programs so they could dole out as much money as possible to as many people as possible. Instead, as a minimal safety net, each county built a house for the poorest of the poor to live in. In order to qualify for residence there, you had to be down to nothing—I mean nothing, not a penny to your name and have nowhere to go; and most often these elderly were sick. Our nearest poorhouse was built by Rockingham County in Wentworth, North Carolina. The structure was a beautiful, old Victorian house that stood as one of the handsomest buildings in the area. Its appearance belied what was on the inside. I have often thought that the county board members must have felt really good about themselves when they rode by that beautiful place they were providing for the poor.

Our MYF group of about fifteen kids ages twelve to sixteen went one cold, stark, Sunday December afternoon to sing for the poor people. I had seen the poorhouse from the outside. It was built near a large county facility. I remember thinking as we drove past that large building on our way to the poorhouse, *That must be where they store our permanent records.* If everything that our teachers and principal told us had really been put into our permanent records, then half of that large building must have been filled with the permanent records of Jimmy Pruitt, Curtis Richmond, and LaVerne Thornton. I have already told you about my permanent record in another story.

As we approached the poorhouse, I thought, *I have never in my young life ever seen such a pretty house, never mind having ever been inside one.* Once we walked inside, my enthusiasm quickly subsided and gloom swept over me. I had been in houses with only a few pieces of worn-out and broken furniture, but these were the most Spartan furnishings that I had ever seen. There were Coca-Cola, RC Cola, and Nehi Cola benches to sit on and little else in the living room. The kitchen had a long, homemade, wooden table with not even a cheap, old-fashioned oilcloth on it. The chairs were mismatched and some were broken. We were shown a few of the bedrooms. There was nothing in most bedrooms except several iron, single beds with thin-striped mattresses. At least the place was clean. I suppose the residents were too poor to generate trash. The residents wore little more than patched rags. To top it off, there was barely any heat in the building on that cold, stark, December day about sixty years ago.

The time came for our Methodist Youth Fellowship to sing in that beautiful Victorian poorhouse. My mother always told me that I was a sensitive child. I knew she felt this way, so I could, on cue, turn on the tears when threatened with a punishment. It almost always worked with Mama. That day the sensitivity was for real. I was in an emotional state and on the verge of tears. We started to sing, and my usually monotone singing voice uttered little more than guttural squeaks. The same happened for other singers who were usually very good. None of

the residents appeared to be entertained by us; they didn't smile or clap. They were required to be there also. I left the poorhouse knowing full well why Mama didn't want to wind up there. I think our annual trek to sing in the poorhouse was for the sole purpose of teaching us a lesson. If that was the reason, I learned my lesson well.

That Sunday night I ate very little supper. Mama heard me heaving while brushing my teeth. She came running and asked, "LaVerne, are you sick?"

"Naw, Mama; the lye soap made me heave."

"The lye soap?"

"Yes, ma'am."

"Are you brushing your teeth with lye soap?"

"Yes, ma'am."

"Why on earth are you brushing your teeth with lye soap?"

"'Cause I want to save money on toothpaste so we won't wind up in the poorhouse." Mama held me and cried. I don't remember her mentioning winding up in the poorhouse again.

Momisms took on a whole new meaning after that.

Low-Hanging Fruit

A dear friend of my family, Janet Whitehead, asked me to do the eulogy for her husband Jerry's funeral recently. It was a very humbling experience that gave me comfort. I shared the podium with a retired minister, Craig Dodson. During the service Rev. Dodson spoke of how our friend had worked for him when he was president of the chain of large discount stores, Maxway. He shared with us that Jerry, knowing that he was dying, asked him to come and minister to him. Rev. Dodson said it was always good to be called in by willing folks to minister to them. He referred to a situation like this as "low-hanging fruit."

I believe it was the first time I had heard that expression since I left the farm. I immediately related it to my childhood. I recalled my dad using that expression. I vividly remember Dad saying, "I will leave the low-hanging fruit for you kids." Applied to picking fruit, it is very obvious what the expression means. The same words were used to define more subtle and nuanced situations. Growing food on the farm was extremely labor intensive back in the forties and fifties. Any food that was easily gathered and prepared was referred to as "low-hanging fruit."

A variety of low-hanging fruits grew in the Bend. Some of these were black walnuts, hickory nuts, hazelnuts, and chestnuts. The only requirements to enjoy these nuts were to gather them off the ground after they matured and fell from the tree, crack them between two rocks, and eat them. Store them in a dry place, and they will last all winter. My mother was a great roaster of all kinds of nuts. They were a wonderful snack on a cold winter's night or to be discovered, by surprise, in our school lunch sacks.

We kept black walnuts stored under a shelter by the corncrib. We had a huge stone lying nearby to use as a cracking surface. Each of us kids had our own small nut-cracking rock. You hold the walnut on top of the large rock and crack down on it with the small one. This process results in many mashed fingers. The ideal way for retrieving the goody out of the cracked walnut was simply by using the loop end of a lady's bobby pin. Years later I found a bobby pin on my office floor. I showed it to my secretary and said, "Someone lost a goody picker." I never got that one fully explained to her.

Some other low-hanging fruits on the farm were greens. Some greens that grew wild in our fields were creasy greens, poke salad, and dandelions. Pick 'em, cook 'em, and eat 'em. They

came to us comparatively easy considering the work usually required for growing food. There are enough edible wild plants around to fill books. Most of the really old people during my childhood knew all the edible ones in our area. I have forgotten the names of some of the plants that we ate from our fields and woods because there were an abundance of them. Poke salad was popularized in 1969 in a song by Tony Joe White and later recorded by Elvis Presley titled "Poke Salad Annie."

If eating dandelions turns you off, try *Taraxacum officinale*. That's what gourmet cooks call dandelions. Wine was made from dandelions by some of our neighbors. Next time you are talking to your favorite wine man ask, "Do you have *Taraxacum officinale* wine?" Tell him it comes from low-hanging fruit in a region of Virginia called the Bend. It has a bouquet reminiscent of warm possum breath and an aftertaste comparable to fermented coon pee.

Berries of many varieties grew wild in the Bend, particularly in the flat area along the river referred to as the low grounds or the river bottoms. Huckleberries, dewberries, blackberries, mulberries, and elderberries were a few of the more popularly grown varieties. All of these berries were eaten raw, used in cobblers, jellied, preserved, and used to make wine. Most berries literally do grow low, and picking them is usually a job for the kids. Sometimes the mothers would visit one another and of course bring along the kids. I hated it when one of the mothers would bring along her little girl with whom I would have to play. If it was dewberry or black-berry picking time, they would often say, "Let's give the kids some buckets and have them pick us a mess of blackberries for a cobbler."

That request was usually a prelude to conflict. Arguments ensued over every aspect of berry picking. Who gets which bucket? Who picks from the first choice bush, the most berry-laden one? We fought over everything that kids can find to fight over when they really don't want to play or pick berries together. Before we left for berry picking, our mothers would soak yarn strings in kerosene and tie one around each wrist and one around each ankle. That worked really well for the chiggers. They could tell by the smell what part of your body to avoid. Not many pictures exist of me as a child, but the ones available show me scratching chiggers with both hands and both feet while scratching my back on a post. I was about thirty years old the first time I went to New York City, and I remembered that it was berry picking time back in the Bend. I took one look at the Empire State Building and wondered, *Do you think that chiggers can get all the way up there?*

One day James and Bobby Hazelwood and I were sent huckleberry picking with my sister Elaine and Jamie Hyler. Bobby started to sing, "Me and my girl went huckleberry hunting; she fell down and I got sumpin." Jamie told her mother, and to our delight, that episode mercifully put an end to coed berry picking.

We boys thought, *Where has that song been all our lives?* Bobby exclaimed that not having to pick berries with the girls made having his mouth washed out with lye soap very worthwhile. We wondered what other value might be derived from that tune.

Now there were some low-hanging fruits on the farm that were literally fruits such as muscadines, damsons, fox grapes, and small sour grapes that we called possum grapes. The humble crabapple grew prolifically in the Bend and found its way to the table in many forms. The grapes were used in all the same way that berries were used. The Hazelwood boys and I tried every way we could think of to make wine but could never get the hang of it. The closest we got to making real wine was a concoction that we would puke up before we could get the promised buzz.

You can bet that Daddy had us take advantage of all the low-hanging fruit, leaving nothing to waste, and providing us kids with much useful exercise and homespun experiences. His philosophy was this: "Gather it in. It won't go to waste. The hogs will eat what we don't. Y'all didn't have anything else to do anyway."

Another time I heard the expression "low-hanging fruit" used was by another good ol' boy who grew up on a farm in Alabama. He was a salesman for the Caterpillar Corporation. At the time I was the main sales contact for my and my partners' engineering and construction company, Wagester Walker Thornton. He was a seatmate on a plane flight. He told me that he was on the way to call on a company that had ordered six bulldozers over the phone. He was going there to work out the specs. He told me in a real Alabama southern accent, "An order that falls on you like that is some kinda real low-hanging fruit."

I often wonder how those old country sayings spread around so well. Must be that a profound statement like "low-hanging fruit" just ought not to stay on a remote farm in Virginia or Alabama.

Kisses and Fried Apple Pies

The Dixes, tenant farmers who lived two farms over from us, did not have an orchard, so we shared our orchard fruits with them. They had a girl one year older than I was. When Mrs. Dix visited Mama, I was required to play with little Janey. Up until I was about ten years old, this was an awful thing to experience. My Bend buddies would chide me mercilessly. "Pee Wee is playing with a girl. Are you going to play dolls today, or will you make a playhouse?"

Hermon, who was older and cruder, always said, "Why don't you play doctor with her? I would love to play doctor with Janey Dix."

Playing doctor with Janey Dix sounded sick to me. When I was first required to play with little Janey, she would dominate everything we did. My complaining to Mama was to no avail. Janey had dirt under her fingernails and often smelled of urine. I was taught by my parents not to hate anyone. In my prayers I would promise God that I didn't hate Janey; I only hated to play with her, but if I ever started to hate people, Janey would surely be at the top of my list.

One incident occurred to change my views toward little Janey. It happened while we were processing dried apples. We started the apple gathering and drying routine when she was eight years old and I was seven.

At apple harvest time Mama would process dried apples with Mrs. Dix. Every family in the Bend dried apples to preserve them through the winter. Apples were gathered, peeled, sliced, and placed on a hot tin roof to dry. Janey and I were assigned to pick apples for Mama and Mrs. Dix to peel and slice. After bringing the first batch, Janey and I returned to the orchard for more apples, and eventually we had gathered enough. In the meantime Mama and Mrs. Dix had peeled and sliced enough apples for Janey and me to get started on our next chore, placing the apples on a hot tin roof to dry. We had a corncrib that was oriented to get full sun in the morning on one side and full sun in the afternoon on the other side. The roof was completely unshaded. This was important to protect against contamination from falling tree debris and roosting bird droppings. I would place a ladder against the crib roof, climb up, and lay an old clean bedsheet out on the roof. Next, we would take apples up, bucket by bucket, and spread them out in a thin layer on the bedsheet. We timed the placing of the apples to be finished

just before the roof got really hot in the morning. To catch the afternoon sun, we transferred them over to the other side of the roof just as the sun was shifting. Transferring the apples to the afternoon sun side often required getting on a really hot roof. In the late afternoon when the sun was no longer shining on the apples, we would climb up, gather the dried apples in a bucket, and take them inside to Mama and Mrs. Dix to divide up.

It would have been in the fall of 1947, when I was ten and little Janey was eleven, that a life-changing episode occurred between Janey and me.

Early one late summer morning, Mrs. Dix and little Janey arrived to dry apples with Mama and me. Janey looked different. She was wearing a clean, new feed-sack print dress. Her hair was blonder, curlier, and cleaner than I had ever seen it before. She didn't even have dirt under her fingernails. She smelled like store-bought soap. She even had a ladylike demeanor about her when asking for my opinion about apple picking.

We took our buckets to the orchard, and Janey asked me, "Which tree should we get apples from?" I was suspicious that she was up to something, but we chose the tree that was the easiest to climb and pick apples. Janey, usually first at everything, said, "You go first."

By now, I was really afraid something was up so I said, "Why don't you go first like you always do?"

"I'm not climbing up first because you will look up my dress."

I'm thinking, *What the heck do I want to see up Janey Dix's dress?* As we continued to work, for the first time, I was actually having fun and even laughing with Janey as we gathered apples.

Well, we made it that far just fine with Janey's new persona. The time came for us to retrieve the dried apples from the corncrib roof. I climbed up the ladder first even though I really had begun to wonder what it looked like up Janey's dress. I took the job of walking on the hot tin roof. Janey climbed up the ladder behind me with two empty buckets. She handed me a bucket. I filled the bucket and handed it back to her. She handed me an empty bucket, took the full one down, and brought up another bucket. We continued this routine until all the apples were gathered. I handed the last bucket to Janey and prepared to follow her down the ladder. Janey stood there at the top of the ladder grinning and said, in a teasing voice, "I ain't letting you down lessen' you kiss me first." My first reaction was to kick her off the ladder. Kissing girls was not on my list of favorite things to do. I had just been through a bad "kissing my sister" episode.

Mama had a practice that humiliated me into submission. If I ever did something that I should not have done to any of my sisters, Mama would make me tell them I was sorry and then make me kiss them on the cheek. I had faced that situation recently. When Mama told me to kiss my oldest sister Betty Jean, I refused, saying, "I will say I'm sorry, but I ain't never going to kiss her again."

I think Mama didn't like my attitude; she got red in the face and said, "If you don't kiss her, I am going to beat the life out of you."

I defiantly answered, "Beat the life outta' me 'cause I ain't gonna kiss her."

Mama grabbed a huge stick that was used to stir stuff in the old black iron pot, held it as one would hold a baseball bat, drew back, and said, "Well, if that is what you want, here goes."

I kissed my sister as fast as lubricated lightning. I learned not to challenge Mama ever again.

There I was, squatting on the roof of the corncrib, staring at a teasing Janey Dix. I started thinking, *This wasn't a bad day; actually it was kinda fun, and besides, Janey looked cute with her new look and all.* So I decided to kiss her hurriedly on the cheek.

She scolded me, saying, "Naw, not like that. Kiss me on the lips like I saw in the picture shows." I hesitated and Janey said, "You ain't getting down 'less you do."

I closed my eyes and kissed little Janey right on the lips. It wasn't as bad as I expected. In fact, it was kind of nice. Truth is, I really liked it. It certainly wasn't a long kiss. I opened my eyes to see Janey hurrying down the ladder. She ran to the house with her bucket of apples, and I followed with mine.

When we were both in the house, our mothers asked if we had fun working together. We both answered, "Yes, Mama."

It must have been a terrible kiss for her because she never asked me to kiss her again, even though I still respected her in the morning.

That was the last time we dried apples together. Just as I was getting interested in some serious kissing, the Dixes moved out of the area and I never saw little Janey Dix again, but I will never forget that first kiss. It sure was better than kissing my sister.

The dried apples were used to make fried apple pies or, as some people called them, half-moon pies. This southern delicacy is loved by everyone. I would like to have one right now. How about you? Here is Mama's favorite recipe for fried apple pies.

FRIED APPLE PIES
2 cups dried apples
2 cups cold water
⅛ tsp. salt
2 cups sugar
1 Tbsp. cinnamon
4 cups flour
Lard for frying

Cook the dried apples in a saucepan with water and the salt. When apples are soft and pulpy, add the cinnamon. Simmer until water is cooked away. Make dough the consistency of pie crust. Roll out and cut into eight-inch circles. Place generous portions of the mixture on half of the dough rounds. Fold the other half of the dough circle over and crimp the edges tightly together with the back of fork tines. Melt lard in a black iron skillet and place the half-moon pies into the hot lard. Turn often until the pies are browned on both sides. Eat immediately.

You may use a healthier fat than lard, but then your fried apple pies won't taste as good as Mama's.

Putting Food on the Table

There is a Food Lion grocery store less than a mile from our home. On a hot July day I got in my air-conditioned truck and rode there to purchase a few grocery items. Among the items I bought were two small potatoes, enough for a meal, along with other vegetables for Lucille and me. We keep our portions small so as to avoid overeating. When I took the potatoes out of the bag and laid them on the counter, I studied them in a way that I had not done in a long time. I have been writing stories about my childhood growing up on the farm in that geographical oddity called "the Bend." Doing so has caused me to look more carefully at things associated with my raising. Being of Irish descent, we grew potatoes as a staple in our diet. This was true for everyone I knew in the Bend, but oh, how different it was putting potatoes on the table back then growing up on the farm. The things I noticed about the two potatoes on the kitchen counter were the eyes. The eyes are the indented spots that, if the potato is left in a dark place for awhile, will develop sprouts. My mind started to drift back to how we farm families put potatoes on our dinner tables.

Each spring, a spot was chosen for the gardens to be planted. Daddy practiced rotating our garden crops, rarely planting the same stuff in the same spot two years in a row. Land for all vegetable gardens was prepared in a similar manner, but this account will follow the process of growing potatoes. Once the field was chosen, a mule- or horse-drawn turning plow was used to turn the soil. This process left the field with huge clods of dirt forming a rough surface. Next, manure was taken from the cow stalls and spread evenly on the freshly turned soil. A mule- or horse-drawn disk harrow was then run back and forth over the soil to break up the clods and smooth the surface of the field, continually working the manure into the ground. Finally, a drag harrow was pulled back and forth through the field, leveling and smoothing the soil even more as the final preparation for planting.

The potato field may have been left in this condition for a few days until Daddy interpreted the moon phase displayed in the *Old Farmer's Almanac* (published continuously since 1792) and decided that the time for planting was right. A supply of potatoes was kept in reserve from the previous crop to be used as seed potatoes. If the potatoes, through rot or other reasons, were

not suitable as seed, we could always buy seed potatoes at the farmers' supply store in Danville. On planting day the women and children prepared the potatoes for planting. The potatoes were cut into small chunks. The cut had to be made in such a way as to have one of the little eyes in each piece. The eye would sprout and grow out of the soil to become a new potato plant. The small chunk of potato left with the eye furnished moisture and nourishment for the plant until it could live off the sun, fertilizer, and soil. While the women and children were cutting the seed potatoes, the men were out using a horse- or mule-drawn single-shovel plow to cut parallel furrows in the soil, forming rows. They then put store-bought fertilizer in the furrow with a mule- or horse-drawn distributor. Next, the whole family was involved in dropping the potato pieces about one foot apart in the furrows. The potatoes were then covered. Usually, this was done with a hand hoe so as to cover them to the proper depth. As the young potato plants emerged from the soil, several plowings with a three-footed, horse-drawn cultivator was done to keep soil built up around the plants as they grew taller. The new potatoes would form in these mounds of soil.

My daddy would not allow a single weed or a blade of grass to grow in our crops, so while the potato vines were growing, the whole family was involved in keeping grass and weeds chopped out of the field. I got in trouble once when I was a kid for insulting a neighbor who had a cornfield that adjoined our potato field. He allowed grass and weeds to grow tall and thick in his cornfield. I made a huge cardboard sign that read, "Keep off the grass!!! Corn is planted under it!!!!!!" It was not hard for the neighborhood to figure out who did it. I lived it down and pretended to be ashamed of my act while I thoroughly enjoyed being asked about it over at Mr. Walter Smart's store.

So the potatoes thrived until these luscious green vines produced beautiful white and pink flowers. Sometime shortly after the blooms started to die, Mama would go out to the field with a small digging tool and dig a mess of new potatoes. Mama would almost always take just one of us kids with her on garden chores. This provided a time for her to teach us valuable skills and lessons about life. I still recall these trips to the garden with Mama. For awhile we

would have new potatoes prepared in every way that farm women knew. Butter was always in the recipes. The butter took a work-intensive, arduous route to the table also. Oh, by the way, we did not have iPods or text messaging. All we had was conversation while gardening with Mama. I wonder how many valuable lessons are lost to electronic white noise today. I wonder what harm is done with mothers shopping at the mall while the kids are playing computer games and listening to some rapper sing about "bitches" and "hos."

After the potato vines totally died, we plowed them up. Again, the old mule or horse was hooked to a turning plow, which was pulled straight down the middle of the row to throw the mound of soil to the right and then to the left, turning up the potatoes. The entire family would rake through the dirt with hand-held potato rakes, pick up the potatoes, and pitch them into a pile. We then took a wagon through the field and piled the potatoes onto the wagon. The freshly dug potatoes were dried in the shade for awhile and then cleaned and put into the burlap bags that had contained fertilizer. Then they were stored in a cool, dry place to provide food for winter. Daddy and I would go down occasionally, pour the potatoes out, pick out the ones that were spoiling, throw them out, and rebag the good ones.

Daddy insisted that we always plant more than our family would need. We had just come through the Great Depression, and Daddy said that you never knew when a neighbor or a relative might come on hard times and maybe we could help out.

Sitting before a bowl of potatoes that you have labored over so much gives a person a different perspective on food. I remember having such a meal once when my youngest sister Brenda, after having helped pick up potatoes for her first time, got a potato from the serving bowl and proudly said, "This is one I picked up."

We children started to kid her unmercifully. Mama intervened and said, "It certainly is one you picked up, and it is a beauty." We got her cue.

With a lot of care, potatoes may last from one crop year to the next, thereby providing food year-round. Blight hit the potatoes in Ireland from 1845 to 1851, wiping out much of those harvests. The crop of potatoes didn't last to the next season and caused mass starvation among the Irish potato people. My grandmother, Shotgun Essie, told me that her grandmother was exiled from Ireland for stealing strawberries from the landlord during this time. She was put on a cattle boat and sent to America. If Shotgun Essie's grandmother had not stolen those low-hanging fruit and had not been sent to America, then surely I would not have been born and you would not be enjoying these glimpses into the unique lifestyles and the lost culture of the Bend People.

On a typical winter's evening, my family sat down to a meal of canned green beans, pork chops, creamed potatoes, and corn bread. We were having milk to drink and fried apple pies—or as some people call them, apple turnovers—for dessert. Putting green beans on the table required about the same process as the potatoes did. The corn was also grown that way, and then we had it ground in order to make the corn bread. The pork came from hogs that we fed twice a day until slaughtering time. Hog-killing day would always be on a cold, late fall day and would require a grueling eighteen hours of hard labor. Apples for the turnovers were picked from our orchard, peeled, sliced, and dried on the metal barn roof. An old bedsheet was laid on the roof facing the sun. The sliced apples were spread out on the sheet to dry. The apples were reoriented throughout the day so as to follow the sun. The milk had come from our cows that very morning. Every ingredient in that delicious meal except the salt and pepper was raised, harvested, and prepared by our own hands. The leftovers were collected in a container and saved for our hogs' next meals. Never was a morsel of food wasted at our home.

When I was growing up, kids always ate at the last table setting when we had company. By the time we got to eat, the best of everything may be gone. My daddy had a brother who lived in New Jersey. Once each summer, Uncle Roy, his fat wife, their son, and a fat couple would visit and stay a week. They were the biggest eaters on earth, ever. We kids called them the "rubber guts." Mama started to hide food to be brought out for us kids after the rubber guts had cleaned the bowls.

After all the work involved in raising food was through, the horses and mules were not put on a shelf 'til we needed them again. Tending farm animals required daily attention year-round. Repeat the aforementioned procedures for each one of the many vegetables we grew on the farm, and you get an idea of what putting food on the table was like for farm families. It's a little more complicated than riding to Food Lion in an air-conditioned truck.

Little Jimmy Dickens recorded the following song about potatoes. The words certainly ring true to me.

TAKE AN OLD COLD 'TATER (AND WAIT)
(Bartlett)

When I was a little boy around the table at home
I remember very well when company would come
I would have to be right still until the whole crowd ate
My Mama always said to me, "Jim, take a 'tater and wait."
Now 'taters never did taste good with chicken on the plate
But I had to eat 'em just the same
That is why I look so bad and have these puny ways
Because I always had to take an old cold 'tater and wait.
And then the preachers they would come to stay awhile with us
I would have to slip around and raise a little fuss
In fear that I would spill the beans or break the china plate
My Mama always said to me, "Jim, take a 'tater and wait."
chorus:
Well I thought that I'd starve to death before my time would come
All that chicken they would eat and just leave me the bun
The feet and neck were all that's left upon the china plate
It makes you pretty darn weak to take an old cold 'tater and wait.

Milking Cows

There exists a special bond between farm folks and their animals. Farm animals both provide food for the family and, when I was growing up on the farm, provided the power for the farm equipment that tilled the soil. We sat down for breakfast and ate eggs from our chickens, bacon or ham from hogs we raised, and milk gravy from our cow's milk, which also provided the butter for our bread. The bread was made from wheat we raised. Mules and horses were the main sources of power to raise all the vegetables that we ate. We only purchased salt, sugar, coffee, and a few other things that we couldn't raise. We kids did many of the chores that put food on our table. My first farm chore was churning milk to make butter and buttermilk. I started doing this chore at four years old.

The closest bond existed between farmers and the milk cows, which require daily attention. We gave our milk cows names, and they responded to them. When a farm family slid into deep poverty, the last thing they gave up was their milk cow.

Farm animals were traded in a market called a livery stable. All farming towns had at least one. Ours was in Danville, Virginia, and was owned and operated by Mr. Witcher. Mr. Witcher was a tight, shrewd businessman known to take advantage of people in need. He would loan poor farmers money on a farm animal, much as a small loan shark loans people money secured by their car. If the poor farmer didn't pay up when he sold his tobacco in the fall, Mr. Witcher would take his animal that secured the loan. His interest rates were unmerciful. Most of his borrowers were tenant farmers and were down to owning only a milk cow. My dad asked Mr. Witcher once, "Have you ever found it in your heart too difficult to repossess someone's animal?"

Mr. Witcher said, "Yes." It happened once when he went to take a cow that was the only possession of a really poor tenant farmer. Mr. Witcher said that while he was loading the cow onto his truck, a little girl in diapers came running up with milk on her lips. Even old hard-hearted Mr. Witcher had tears in his eyes as he told my dad, "I unloaded that cow and left."

One of the chores required when owning cows was twice-daily milking. I started milking when I was about twelve years old. I learned right away that cows have a sense of humor. They like to tease humans. A cow leaves the barn in the morning looking for cockleburs to fill her

tail. They do this so they can slap you in the face while you are milking. They also look for wild onions to eat. They know that onions will make their milk smell and taste bad. The cow will approach the barn with a subtle grin on her fat lips after a successful day in the pasture eating wild onions and gathering cockleburs on her tail.

My first experience at milking came one afternoon when my dad said to me, "You should be strong enough to milk now, so I want you to take on the milking chore."

I was sent to the barn with a milk pail and a stool. I had watched my father milk enough times that I knew the basics. As in most cases, when you observe a talented person at work, you often miss the subtleties involved in their skills. I led the cow into the barn and put a measured amount of grain in the feeding trough. The cow gladly started to chew on the grain. That was the only way in which that cow cooperated. I then placed the three-legged stool on the right side of the cow. I always wondered why the right side. Although I was somewhat rebellious as a youngster, I never got up the nerve to milk a cow from the left side. I have been left-handed from the womb. No amount of warnings and hand slapping worked to convert me. I sat on the stool, placed the milk pail on the barn floor under the cow, and nudged the cow to move her hind right foot back, giving easy access to the milk sack and the four associated long nipples. Once the cow's posture was correct, I started to extract the milk from the bag into the milk bucket. I started by pinching the tit between my thumb and forefinger at the spot where the tit joins the bag. I then started a downward rolling squeeze, thereby forcing the milk trapped in the tit to come out and into the bucket. At this point the cow started to employ every maneuver known to cows. To resist my efforts, Old Bessie first kicked the bucket over. Then she slapped my face with her cocklebur-laden tail. The third act of defiance was to pee. There is an old southern saying, "They scattered like the pee from a cow pissing on a flat rock." Well, a cow peeing on a hard, dirt, barn floor goes everywhere, too, including into the milk pail. I ran crying to the house with an empty milk pail, bloody scratches on my face, and cow pee all over me. I had left Old Bessie eating grain with a grin on her big, fat, bitchy cow lips.

My dad consoled me and said, "I knew you would have trouble your first time, but I wanted to get your attention. Now tomorrow I will show you how to milk a cow, and you will surely watch and listen." My dad had a way of narrowing the scope down when teaching a lesson. Dad always let you know first what you didn't know about something. Thus, he had identified the starting point of the learning experience.

The next day at milking time my dad went to the barn with me. Unlike when I went alone, Bessie seemed pleasant and somewhat delighted to go into the barn. Dad told me to watch carefully every move he made. I learned that day the truly perfect cow-milking technique. Daddy's performance was symphonic. He and Bessie were in a remarkable harmony.

Here is Dad's technique the way I explained it to a woman from New Jersey years later. In the 1960s, I worked for a company that encouraged young management people to get additional education. I learned about a school operated by the American Management Association in New York City. I wanted more education and loved to go to New York. Since the company paid for it all, what more could I ask? I took several courses at the school, which were usually taught by professors from the business departments of Ivy League colleges. More often than not I was the only southerner in the class. Obviously, I got plenty of kidding about my accent. I usually spread it on thickly and had fun with it all. This gave me undivided attention every time I spoke. It was like the old E. F. Hutton TV ad: "When E. F. Hutton talks, people listen." In my case they probably didn't give a damn about what I was saying. They wanted to hear how I said it. Well, at one lunch we had six other people at our table, four men and two women, all Yankees. A buxom lady from New Jersey put on a fake southern accent and asked, "And so are you all from the South?"

"Yes, ma'am," I replied.

"Did you all grow up on the farm?"

"Yes, ma'am," I said.

"You all ever milk cows?" she inquired.

"Yes, ma'am," I responded.

Everyone was listening and knew that she was making fun of me, and they were waiting for my angry response. They didn't get an angry response. I instead beamed and asked her, "Would you all like me to tell you all how to milk a cow?" All this flowery language got everyone's attention and they seemed genuinely interested in what I might say, so I started to explain how to milk a cow as my dad had shown me so many years ago.

"First, you greet the cow at the barn door with a smile and ask, 'How was your day? Did you find lush green grass? Was the water clean and cool? Did you have problems with the other animals?' As she passes by on her way into the barn, you gently stroke and pat her behind.

You then step ahead of her and put grain into the feeding trough. If she moos and moos, you just listen patiently without interruption. Next, you place a milk pail under her and put your milking stool on the barn floor." Using hand motions to simulate the actions used in milking and lowering my voice, I explained the remainder of the process. "Once you are seated on the stool, you very gently and slowly stroke the inside of her right rear thigh. The cow gladly moves her leg back, opening up access to her milk bag."

I looked at the woman's rather substantial bosom and said, "Ma'am, unlike you, with two tits with a nipple on each one, a cow has one huge tit with four very long, sensuous nipples. It is important to be slow and gentle with the cow at this point as you would be with a woman. With both hands cupped you stroke the entire bag, lifting it and lowering it; then using four fingers on each hand, you slowly stroke in a circular motion the entire bag. Next, you slowly and gently rub each nipple with your thumb and forefinger tips for several minutes. You wind up gently squeezing the tip of her nipples. All the while you are talking softly to her. The cow should be ready now to give it up—the milk that is." By now you could hear a pin drop. "New Jersey's" face was flushed, her breath was rapid, and she squirmed slightly in her seat. I never really got to how you squeeze the milk out of the nipple.

I think I heard "New Jersey" say to the woman beside her, "I could like farm boys."

As the lunch ended I asked, "If you all have time this week, would you all like for me to tell you all about castrating bulls?"

Oh, by the way, I was never kidded again about being a southern boy. Several people wanted to buy my dinner that week.

Making Molasses

Very early in my life we made molasses. Molasses was made from stalks of sorghum cane, which in the field look like small stalks of corn. The cane stalks were harvested at their peak of juiciness. The stalks were chopped down, gathered in bundles, and brought by a mule-drawn wagon to the "'lasses-making place." The 'lasses-making place consisted of a juice press and a boiling vat.

The cane press had a huge wooden tub containing a platen, which is a flat metal plate, attached to a screw. The screw passed through a bearing attached to a permanently mounted cross member above the tub. A long pole was affixed to the top of the screw. When the long pole was rotated, the platen would travel down the screw, thus squeezing the juice from the stalks that were chopped and placed in the tub. The mule was harnessed to the long pole as the source of power. The mule would walk in a circle around the entire contraption. The juice ran out the bottom of the tub through a chute to the vat. When a sufficient amount of juice was in the vat, a fire was built under it. The juice was boiled to drive off the excess water, leaving molasses. The molasses was jarred after cooling enough to be handled.

The mule is a hybrid of a jackass and a horse. Nature extracted the most awful traits from each animal and deposited them in the mule. The mule's head is about 99 percent granite. The remainder is something akin to a brain. When I was about eight years old, I would help Daddy lead a milk cow to a neighbor's bull. Thus, I learned at the young age of eight how calves were made. I also saw in this procedure something involved that I would grow to like someday. I asked Daddy why we never led the mules to do that. Daddy said mules can't do that. I thought, *What the hell animal on earth would want to do that to a mule anyhow?*

To me, making molasses was as close as it gets to living with the food chain. When we first sampled this new molasses, I wanted nothing but molasses that I helped make, with butter that I churned, and corn bread from the corn that I helped to grow, harvest, and grind. From time to time Mama would have to wean me off my molasses diet; after a few days with violent tremors, I would be fine.

Doesn't this paint a pastoral image in your mind? Poor little, towheaded, barefooted, south-ern farm kids, harvesting sorghum cane, firing up the old molasses vat, and harnessing the faithful ol' mule to make molasses. All the while these kids are laughing and singing, "She'll Be Coming 'round the Mountain When She Comes" and "One Hundred Bottles of Beer on the Wall." Conjures up kind of a *Sound of Music* scene, doesn't it? Makes you want to rush to Food Lion and buy some molasses, doesn't it?

Here's the problem: Mules don't say, "Please, may I be excused; I have to go in the woods and do numbers one and two." Mules let go when the need arises, paying no attention to their whereabouts. Mules don't mind walking around in that circle all day in what they have voided and excreted. The squeezed cane pulp has to be discarded in a pile nearby. The boiling molasses creates a sticky scum that has to be constantly raked off the surface of the mix and thrown out. Molasses is like diesel fuel. You get a drop on your fingertip and in thirty minutes it's in your ears and between your butt cheeks. So it is with molasses. By noon you are sticky all over. All these things go on while smoke billows up from the wood fire. This mix attracts flies from as far away as Argentina. Word gets out in the wilderness, "Come all vermin and enjoy." Some species of vermin appear that have probably not been classified to this day. About a week after molasses-making time, buzzards would circle over the site. Not even a starving buzzard would risk landing and pecking through that vile heap. I saw a buzzard touch down on molasses residue once. After one whiff, he tore off so fast that he passed a bat out of hell.

Has your image of making and eating molasses changed?

When I was about thirty-two years old, I was plant manager of a company that made terra-cotta sewer pipe. My plant was at the crossroads named Gulf in North Carolina. At one time, we were investigating the purchase of another company. Three hotshots from Ohio flew to Sanford in a private plane to meet with us concerning the acquisition. They were an arrogant, condescending lot. Seeing nothing industrial or commercial around us, the haughtiest one asked, "Is there anything at all around here to see or do?"

It just so happened that several of our employees took off work one day every year to make molasses. I knew their location. I had been there the previous year in an attempt to explain to them that they lost several hundred dollars in wages to stay out of work to make about thirty dollars worth of molasses. That mattered nothing to them. Making molasses the old-fashioned way was a family tradition and, by damn, make molasses they would. Anyway, I answered the man's question by telling him about the molasses industry we had in Gulf. He called his pilot and explained that he would have to file a new flight plan. He explained that Mr. Thornton had arranged for a tour of a molasses plant.

Imagine the looks on their faces when we arrived at a scene just like I already described to you. They all three looked ill. One said, "My grandfather ate molasses for his health every day until the day he died. I am sure glad he never saw it being made."

The other two never spoke again except to issue a feeble, "Nice meeting you," as they boarded their plane for the trip back to the socially advanced state of Ohio. Those three men left North Carolina with everything they ever thought about the South having been confirmed.

There is a sanitized version of our molasses on the market today called Grandma's Molasses. I keep a jar in the cupboard all the time. If I ever start feeling my oats, I wash my face and hands in lye soap and eat a spoonful of Grandma's Molasses. I get instant humility.

Strange Edibles

Lucille and I recently visited Charleston, South Carolina. We stayed two nights in the Francis Marion Hotel. Inquiring as to where to find a really good lunch place, we were told to try the Hominy Grill. We were told that it was only a short walk from the Francis Marion. Since the person giving us directions was young and athletic looking, we chose to drive. The restaurant was okay, but we presumed that the lad who made the recommendation must have been the son of the owner. However, it was a most memorable experience, not for the food, but for the chain of thoughts it started in my mind. I grew up making and eating hominy. All the way home I thought, *When I get home, I am going to make hominy.* After we returned home, I reviewed in my mind the recipe for making hominy. Since we had none of the ingredients needed to make this delightful and delicious dish, Lucille reminded me with a frown that we had once bought hominy in the grocery store on one of my previous fits of nostalgia.

When we arrived home, I immediately rushed to Food Lion. I searched for awhile, but my impatience got to me and I asked an employee where I could find the hominy. He replied, "Hunh?"

The next employee asked, "Hominy, what the heck is hominy?"

Eventually, on my own I found the hominy—two cans, covered with dust, at the bottom of a shelf under the regular corn. I bought both cans and anxiously waited for that night's dinner. I remembered that Mama used to fry it in a frying pan with a large amount of lard and a generous portion of salt and pepper. Having weaned myself off lard many years ago, I chose instead to use extra virgin olive oil. After the olive oil got hot, I sprinkled salt and pepper and put in the hominy. After the hominy browned, I raked the gummy mix into a bowl. I have forgotten what I served with the hominy, but I could tell by Lucille's expression that it was not going on our favorites' list. I tasted the hominy, added salt, tasted it, added pepper, tasted it again, and added vinegar. Next I tried nutmeg, and then cinnamon; it got worse. I warmed it over in a Styrofoam bowl for lunch the following day. It was horrible. I poured it out and ate the Styrofoam bowl, which was tastier. I surmised that the lard must have made the difference between Mama's recipe and mine, or my memory of how delicious hominy is resulted from nostalgia. By the way, lard, salt, and pepper on confetti would be tastier.

OLD FASHIONED HOMINY

One late afternoon a long time ago, sitting on Mr. and Mrs. Hazelwood's front porch, I brought up the subject of hominy. They have made hominy many times and remembered their parents and grandparents making it. The following isn't an exact recipe; however, it should be close enough that you could make hominy without much difficulty by following it and using your own good judgment.

One necessary ingredient was lye. To get lye, they used a section of a hollow tree, set it on a base that slanted, and filled the hollow part of the tree section with ashes from the fireplace, wood heater, or cookstove. The very best ashes were green oak ashes. Water was then poured through the ashes. When the water trickled through at the bottom, it was caught in a bucket and poured back through the ashes until the lye water was as strong as they wanted it. They used this lye water to make hominy and homemade soap. Now, you may be able to find concentrated lye in some country stores.

The next step was to soak dry corn in the lye water until the skin and the little tip at the point of the kernel came off. This might take a day or two, and the hominy was stirred occasionally during that time. When the skin came off, the corn swelled, breaking those skins, and then it was washed thoroughly a minimum of ten times to remove all the lye. The last thing to do then was to cook the corn until it was tender, cover it with a generous amount of butter, salt to taste, and "eat up."

If you'd like more detailed information on how to make hominy, homemade soap, or lye, I suggest that you check out this web page: the library.springfield.missouri.org/lochist/periodicals/bittersweet/sp74.htm.

These experiences and conversations concerning hominy caused me to challenge my memories about some of the other strange edibles I consumed while growing up in the Bend. We had souse meat, chitterlings, chicken feet, opossum, pig testicles, and the strangest of all, squirrel brains. The recipes, my commentaries, and my recommendations are included in the rest of the story.

If ever the old saying, "On the farm we ate everything except the squeal," was true about an animal, it would be the hog. Souse meat is the next step above eating the squeal. You literally eat the parts that do the squealing.

SOUSE MEAT

One recipe says to take a dressed hog head and boil it until the meat is falling off. Pull all the meat off the bone: ears, tongue, nose, eyelids, and so on. Mash the meat to as fine a texture as possible. Add salt, pepper, and sage to taste. Add 1½ cups of vinegar per head. Blend the mixture uniformly with a heavy spoon. Pat it flat in shallow pans about one inch deep. Place the pans in the refrigerator overnight so the souse meat will congeal. Cut the congealed meat into squares and serve.

The problem is that it is impossible to get all the hair off a hog's head, especially the ear and nose hairs. While eating souse meat, you invariably get several hog hairs in your mouth and throat, causing you to have violent heaving episodes and causing your tablemates to puke. Souse meat is probably best served after six beers.

My recommendation: Until they can grow a completely hairless hog, bypass the souse meat.

CHITTERLINGS

Chitterlings are, to get right to the point, hog guts. It really makes sense to slaughter a hog, jerk his guts out, and eat them after about a year that the hog has stored fecal matter in his intestines. Chitterlings are readily available in some grocery stores because they are still known as soul food in some quarters. When I was a kid, I stayed overnight with James. They had chitterlings for supper, and James sat across the table from me. During the meal, he raised a piece of chitterling up, peeped through it, and said, "Thornton, I think I see some kernels of corn in there."

Chitterlings are best prepared this way: Wash them many times, boil until tender, remove from the pot, cut in about two-inch sections, batter, and fry them in a pan.

My recommendation: If you must try them, put a bowl of chitterlings beside a bowl of hog manure and say, "Eeny meeny miney moe, catch a gypsy by the toe; if he hollers, let him go, eeny meeny miney moe." Eat the bowl that you are pointing to at the end of the rhyme. You probably won't know the difference.

CHICKEN FEET

Mama didn't cook chicken feet at our home, but two of my aunts did. I don't recall how they were prepared. I do know that Aunt Duddy made a really good chicken soup with them. I suppose that you could substitute a mess of chicken feet in any chicken soup recipe. Aunt C.D.

fried them in some fashion, and they were really tasty. One family I knew broke chicken bones and pushed out the marrow to make bone marrow soup. Hmmmm, sounds appetizing, doesn't it? Here is a favorite chicken feet recipe:

12 chicken feet, declawed and skinned
1 tsp. sugar
3 Tbsp. dark soy sauce
2 Tbsp. rice wine
1 piece orange rind
3 slices ginger
3 green onions
star anise to taste
¼ tsp. pepper
1 pint water
1 Tbsp. barbecue sauce
Directions: Combine all ingredients and simmer for 1½ hours.

My recommendation: Go ahead; try some chicken feet, but be sure to clean between the toes.

OPOSSUM

Opossum was a specialty of my Uncle Crawford. Opossums were plentiful in the Bend, as was all small game. Uncle Crawford would catch one and keep it in a pen for about six weeks. While he had it penned, he would feed it table scraps such as corn and other grains to make it as fat as possible. After the possum was fully fatted, he killed and dressed it. Here's where the problem arose. No woman wanted to cook possum. They are nasty, terribly greasy, and a general mess to deal with. Possum can be prepared all the same ways chicken is prepared. No, it doesn't taste like chicken. It is not bad to the taste, but I haven't had possum since I left the Bend, and I don't plan to have any. I will leave opossum as a quaint memory of mine. Here is a popular opossum recipe:

OPOSSUM AND SWEET POTATOES
1 opossum (about 2½ pounds)
2½ tsp. salt
pepper to taste

½ cup water

4 medium sweet potatoes

2 Tbsp. sugar

flour

Trim excess fat from opossum and discard. Wash quickly inside and out with warm water; drain thoroughly. Rub salt and pepper well into the opossum inside and out. Sprinkle inside and out with flour. Lay the opossum on its back in a roasting pan. Add water, cover, and bake at 350°F until about half-done (45 to 60 minutes). Split peeled potatoes in half lengthwise and place in pan around opossum. Add more water if needed. Cover sliced potatoes and opossum and cook 30 more minutes.

My recommendation: If you are curious about opossum, study them rather than eat them. Here are some facts. The opossum has barely changed since its very ancient history. This is due to two main characteristics. One is their ability, when threatened, to slow their bodily functions down to the point that they are, by all appearances, dead. That is where "playing possum" came from. Many animals of prey will not eat a dead animal. Playing possum provides the opossum with unique protection that has helped them survive for eons. Second, the female opossum has two ports in her vagina. The male opossum has a forked penis that is accommodated by

the female's double entry system. The male's sperm enters the female in pairs. This arrangement prevents other animals from crossbreeding with the opossum. When stripped of all its flesh, the opossum penis is a hard forked bone, a built-in erection support device. Some folks fashioned the opossum penis into watch fobs and key chain fobs. It was really cool in the Bend to have a possum penis key chain fob. Here is a Jeff Foxworthy kind of thing for you: "If you carry a possum-dick watch fob, you could be a redneck!"

Who on earth would want to eat a cute little animal crawling around the forest playing dead and wearing a permanent erection?

PIG TESTICLES

Strange as it may sound, fried pig testicles are delicious. You only need to get past the thought. I was always embarrassed to admit to eating pig testicles until I learned just what a delicacy edible animal's testicles are in our society. At one time I was one of the owners of an engineering and construction company that built animal feed plants. A part of my role in the company was to attend industry conventions. Once I attended a convention in Springdale, Arkansas, hosted by Tyson Foods. There was a reception in a huge hall for approximately five hundred people. I had flown and driven all day to get there and had missed lunch, so I was quite hungry. I loaded my plate at the hors d'oeuvres table. There were some really delicious small meatballs on the table. Meatballs are one of my favorites, so I loaded my plate with mostly meatballs. I soon struck up a conversation with a Tyson engineer who would be instrumental in choosing my company to build a new turkey feed mill for his company.

I commented on the delicious flavor of the meatballs, saying they very well might be the best I had ever had. He thanked me and said, "They are not meatballs; they are turkey nuts." I forced down the remaining four balls, not wanting to insult my host and risk losing the opportunity to build Tyson's new mill. We didn't get the contract for their mill, but by then it was too late to puke up the turkey nuts.

The following is an old family recipe for animal testicles:

Serves 4
2 lbs. pig testicles (lamb/sheep, calf, turkey, or bull testicles can also be used)
1 cup unbleached white flour
¼ cup cornmeal
1 cup red wine
salt, pepper, garlic powder to taste

Louisiana Hot Sauce

lard

Using a sharp knife, split the tough skinlike muscle that surrounds each "oyster." You can remove the skin more easily if the oysters are frozen and then peeled while thawing. Set into a pan with enough salt water to cover them for 1 hour to remove some of the blood and drain.

Transfer to large pot. Add enough water to float the oysters and a generous tablespoon of vinegar. Parboil, drain, and rinse. Let cool and slice each oyster into ¼-inch thick-ovals. Sprinkle salt and pepper on both sides of sliced oyster to taste.

Mix flour, cornmeal, and some garlic powder to taste in a bowl. Roll each slice into this dry mixture. Dip into milk. Dip into dry mixture. Dip into wine quickly (repeat the procedure for a thicker crust). Place into hot cooking oil (it'll sizzle some, so be careful!). Cook until golden brown or tender, and remove with a strainer. (The longer they cook, the tougher they get.)

My recommendation: Go ahead, fry up some pig testicles. You only live once. Mustard or catsup goes well with them if you simply boil them.

SQUIRREL BRAINS

Black walnut, hickory nut, hazelnut, and chestnut trees grew everywhere in the Bend, providing an abundant supply of food for all manner of small game. The squirrel population was particularly prolific. My daddy was an avid outdoorsman who loved to hunt and took pride in his ability to live off the land. He died at sixty-nine still believing it nasty to pee in the house. I'm confident that my daddy could have kept our family fed with a mule and plow, a knife, and a shotgun. He would rather eat roadkill that he harvested himself than filet mignon in a fancy restaurant. Mama didn't always gladly prepare his catch, but knew how to and prepared it willingly whether it came from forest or stream. Many times my daddy would be in the woods before daylight, hunting. He would bring back several squirrels for Mama to cook for breakfast. She boiled them or fried them. When they were boiled, she smothered them in milk gravy. We kids loved to crack the skulls and eat the brains. Here is a favorite squirrel recipe:

6 young squirrels

2 egg yolks

flour

paprika
salt
pepper
garlic powder
onion powder
vegetable oil

Cut squirrels into pieces including the heads and wash well. Beat egg yolks and pour over squirrels. Season flour with spices to taste, and add lots of black pepper. Roll squirrel pieces in flour and fry in oil on medium heat. Cover with lid and cook about 5 minutes on each side; then remove lid to allow squirrels to brown. Crack the skulls and remove the brains for a tasty delicacy.

EASY BROWN GRAVY

Leave about 3 tablespoons of oil in the skillet and add 3 tablespoons of flour, salt and lots of pepper. Brown flour on medium heat and add about 2 cups of water. Turn heat up to high. Let come to a boil and add more water until gravy reaches desired consistency.

My recommendation: If you have a brain, you won't eat squirrel brains.

There were other strange edibles eaten in the Bend, such as coon and crow. We also ate a variety of greens like poke weed, creasy greens, and dandelion. All in all we had a much bigger variety of food growing up in the Bend than we have today. I have noticed lately that you can get prepackaged field greens that include some of the foods I ate growing up.

I hope that this story has given you a glimpse of the fine cuisine and delectable edibles that we enjoyed in the Bend. All these delicious foods can be prepared from my family members' recipes included in this story.

Planting Tobacco and Pilot Mountain

Most of us kids growing up in the Bend never went outside a two-county area—Pittsylvania County, Virginia, and Rockingham County, North Carolina. In fact, this practice applied to most kids in Happy Home School, my local grammar school, which served a large area of Rockingham County as well as us Bend kids. We didn't have TV back then. We did have a battery-operated Philco radio. The radio had two knobs, one for on/off/volume and one for tuning. The antenna was a long wire mounted on poles and extended out about two hundred feet. We had two publications coming into our home: the *Progressive Farmer* magazine and the *Danville Register* newspaper. Through these resources and my schoolwork, I realized that there was a great big world out there. I wondered about, as the old song goes, "Those Far Away Places with Strange Sounding Names." I daydreamed that one day I would "See me some of that big world."

The first recollection I have of doing real farmwork was carrying water to the tobacco planters. First, the tobacco field was plowed, harrowed, and raked level. Next, a turn plow was used to form the rows where the tobacco was to be planted. These rows were shaped to form straight, long ridges about four feet apart. The tobacco plants were set on these ridges.

Tobacco was planted by two methods, depending on whether the ground was wet or dry. If a good rain came near planting day and the ground was wet, the tobacco plants were set with a planting peg. The planting peg was fashioned from heart of pine, referred to by country folks as "lighter wood." It was called "lighter wood" because it contained a high content of turpentine. When split into small pieces, it would light or burn easily and was good to use when starting fires in stoves. It was also abrasion-resistant, making it long-wearing when used as a tobacco planting peg. Planting tobacco with a peg was backbreaking work. We bent over, poked a hole in the listed row, and inserted a tobacco plant in the hole. We used the peg to tamp wet soil around the roots of the plant and moved on about two feet to the next plant position, never rising up.

I have a peg carved by my father that I used until I left the farm for good in 1959. I keep that peg where I can always see it. Occasionally, I take it in my hand, bend down, and simulate planting tobacco. This serves to remind me that I have never really worked as hard physically since I left the farm.

If the young tobacco plants were ready and no rains came, the tobacco was planted with a hand planter. Planting in dry soil required putting in some water with each plant. As you can see in the illustration on the next page, a planter has two cone-shaped pieces with each one open at the top. One worker handles the planter, while a second worker carries a basket of tobacco plants. The large open-top cone is filled with water. The pointed end of the planter is stuck about four inches deep in the listed row. The worker carrying the plants drops a tobacco plant in the small open-top cone. The planter operator squeezes a lever just under the handle at the top. This opens the jaws of the planter and allows the tobacco plant to be left in the soil as the planter is lifted out of the ground. This allows loose dry soil to flow in around the roots of the plant. That cycle is repeated until the entire tobacco field is planted.

As this process is carried out, a constant supply of water is required for the planter. That job is the easiest one at planting time and is usually done by the smallest kids. Barrels of water are strategically placed around the field. The water bearer carries water in whatever size bucket he can handle and delivers it from the barrels to the planter. As I wrote earlier, that was my first real farming chore. For carrying water, the bucket I used was a one-gallon Pilot Knob coffee bucket. My dad never bought anything without figuring on using the leftovers for a useful purpose. Thus, he bought Pilot Knob coffee in the gallon size. When the coffee was used up, we were left with a very handy bucket. The one that became mine had a "bell" or handle for carrying.

I was probably about seven or eight when I carried water to the planters in that Pilot Knob coffee bucket. As a curious child I asked often about the picture on that bucket and was told by my uncle, "Yes, that is a picture of a real place. It is called Pilot Mountain." I vowed that one day I would see that mountain. Time passed, I grew up, and went away to college and pretty much forgot about that picture of Pilot Mountain on that coffee bucket.

I finished college, got a good job, and did start to "See me some of that big world." It was as exciting as I had imagined it would be.

In 1972 I had reason to travel on a business trip along Route 52 North near Winston-Salem, North Carolina. It was a gorgeous fall day. The sky was cornflower blue. The sun from behind me was lighting up the beautiful fall colors. I was already high on the scenery when I looked up and to my left. Unexpectedly, there it was up ahead—Pilot Mountain, the object of my mostly forgotten vow of years ago. I stopped and stared at it for awhile, feeling glad to be alone and not having to explain why I could get so emotional over a simple mountain view.

Now at seventy-two, I have been in all fifty states and in ten foreign countries. I have seen the Swiss Alps, the White Cliffs of Dover, and watched the sun set in Key West, Florida. While I have seen a myriad of breathtaking scenes in all of the United States, I have yet to be more thrilled than I was at that moment when I got my first view of Pilot Mountain.

Mules Cause Cussing

There is an old adage that says, "You can lead a horse to water, but you can't make him drink." The same cannot be said about a mule. The adage written for a mule would go like this, "It may be possible at various times during a mule's life that, the right person, at the right time, under ideal conditions, may lead him to water providing the mule is thirsty." On the way to the water, the leader would probably use the foulest of language and pray for the mule to drown while drinking. What is a mule? The following is a brief description of the mule.

The mule is a cross between a donkey stallion, called a jack, and a horse mare. Hinnies are just the opposite, a stallion horse crossed to a donkey jennet. For all purposes, hinnies and mules are classified and shown together under the general term "mule." A mule or hinny may be a male (horse mule or horse hinny) or a female (mare mule or mare hinny). Sometimes horse mules, the males, are called Johns, and the mares are called Mollies. Both male and female mules have all the correct "parts" but they are sterile and cannot reproduce. A very few (about one in 1 million) mare mules have had foals, but these are very, very rare. No male mule has ever sired a foal. So if you cross a mule to a mule, you get nothing! Mules and hinnies must be bred by crossing a donkey and horse every time. Male mules should also be castrated, since they are sterile. They can become dangerous with too many hormones. You can't show an intact male mule anyway, and it is useless to keep them a stallion.

You males already find inherent flaws in the mule's makeup. Castration is absolutely required if one is to have any control over a mule's behavior. Harnessing a mule with balls would be like lassoing a tornado. Some farmers would actually have their team of mules pull a heavily loaded wagon up a hill a few times to tone the mules down a bit before attempting to plow with them. When you take a mule to the barn at the end of a workday, measure out some grain and throw some hay in the feedbox. You have to admire that strong, hard-working semifreak of nature.

We had a white mule named Molly. Molly had a tough mouth that required what is called a sawtooth bit. The bit is attached to the bridle. It is the bar that goes into the mouth of a

harnessed horse or mule. The guidelines are attached to each end of the bit. When you want the animal to go left, you gently tug on the left line; to stop them you tug back evenly, and so on. A sawtooth bit is designed to apply pain to the mule's mouth when tugged on so as to gain control. In the case with Molly, you jerked hard on the lines if you wanted results. "Stubborn as a mule" is not an idle comment. Someone did research and found that the mule is the baseline for stubborn, followed by its closest contender. . . . Well, I won't say! Molly, as do many mules, had a ticklish spot behind her left front leg just where you hooked up the belly band of the work harness. You had to harness her with extreme caution. If you barely touched her ticklish spot, she would bite you so quickly that avoidance was impossible. I swear that mules love to bite people. You could see a vicious grin on her long, bitchy mule face as she shivered hard enough to undo what you had done applying the harness.

I was trading "growing up as poor farmers" stories with a man from Missouri recently. The subject of mules came up. He allowed as how a mule would be good to you for ten years just waiting for a good chance to kick your butt.

My Uncle Kyle, married to my daddy's sister Aunt Ruth, was bitten by his mule once too often. One day his mule bit him on the shoulder, and Uncle Kyle bit back. Uncle Kyle was seen biting the mule by his son Robert. Uncle Kyle was, as country people would say, slight of build. Robert described how Uncle Kyle, when bitten by the mule, grabbed the mule by its big fat lip with both hands and bit down hard on the mule's lip. The mule jerked her head back so quickly that Uncle Kyle could not release his teeth and hands fast enough and was body slammed against the barn wall. Aunt Ruth said that Uncle Kyle had learned never to bite back at a mule again.

Every farmer in the Bend worked mules singly or in pairs, except us. Daddy paired our mule Molly with a beautiful draft horse named Maude. As long as Molly was teamed with Maude, she worked calmly and was controllable. Maude was a delight to work with. Daddy had bought her from a logging company where she had been used to snake (drag) saw logs out of the woods to be loaded and hauled to the sawmill. Maude loved to work. She seemed to express pure joy at being harnessed up and hooked to something to pull. When Molly was teamed with Maude, she operated with great draft animal decorum. Are you wondering why farmers used mules instead of only horses? Well, in fairness to mules, they have an exceptional ability to balance distance. A mule with a load on its back can walk between two objects and have no measurable difference in the space on either side. They can walk a narrow rocky path along a cliff wall and maintain perfect balance. That is the reason they are used by hiking guides, as in the Grand Canyon, to ferry people safely over treacherous ground. When pulling a plow, it is important to walk right down the middle of the rows, which makes the skilled mule perfectly suited for row crop farming. Thus is needed the skilled mule.

Mules are hay-burning, grain-eating fart factories. When pulling a plow, a mule knows just when to let go of a fart. It is most often just as you are taking in a deep breath. Mules can detect a yawn just in time to fill your lungs with mule fart. They fart in multiples, letting out a string of farts that go longer than a healthy person can hold his breath. It's ninety-five degrees F and suddenly, *whoom, whoom, whoom*, a hot stinking cloud engulfs you. You can't run away but you can't tolerate it either. It is very close to the old problem of the unstoppable force meeting, head-on, the immovable object. There is no solution; it is just all part of farming with mules.

The first plowing job a boy is given on a tobacco farm is called plowing out middles. When tobacco is about a foot tall, it is "laid by." This expression, I believe, comes from the fact that this is the last intense working of the soil around the tobacco plants before the harvest begins. After laying by tobacco, there is a period of ease before harvesting. During this period you can just lie by or relax some. When tobacco is laid by, a turn plow is used to throw soil up around the plants. Throwing the soil from the middle to the right side of the row and then from the middle to the left side of the row leaves a mound of soil in the middle that needs to be plowed level. This is done with a three-footed cultivator or a strange-looking plow called a buzzard wing.

When I was assigned my first plowing job, I was about thirteen years old. I was to plow out middles. Dad harnessed up Maude, and I was expecting to use her. Daddy looked at me and said, "You harness up Molly and hook her to that three-footed cultivator when we get to the field." Not liking how things were shaping up, I still did as I was told without grumbling.

Daddy started ahead to lay the tobacco by. He had to get a row or two ahead before I started, since he had to plow two furrows to my one. This allowed me to take it slowly to learn my new job. After a few trips through the tobacco field, I was getting the hang of it. As usual, after awhile, I thought that I knew it all. I caught up with Daddy and took the time to take my shirt off so I could get a tan. I put the plow lines around my lower back to avoid getting a farmer's tan. I got to the end of the first row after taking my shirt off. As I dragged the plow around and lined it up to go down the middle of the next row, the hook on the singletree and trace chains came loose from the plow. Molly continued on, trapping me between the plow handles. At this point Molly was pulling me, with her mouth carrying the entire load. Suddenly, I was pivoted into the air and sort of pole vaulted up. All that pressure on Molly's mouth still did not stop her. By the time I fell to the ground, I had been dragged with the plow lines trapped under my armpits. The load on Molly's jaws finally caused her to stop. I never noticed that Daddy was approaching the end of the field two rows over. I let out a string of profanity, utilizing every word I had ever heard from Uncle Luther and Uncle Crawford's fox-hunting friends. My string of words would be the envy of a Russian sailor. Since my voice was still changing, I am sure the cussing had a melodic, yodeling sound. I glanced up and saw Daddy. I immediately prayed, "God, if you won't let Daddy kill me, I will never call your name in vain again."

Daddy never commented. Ignoring the whole affair, he turned around and went about his work. For the remainder of the day, I called on every skill I could summon to become a good plowboy. I wondered when the hammer would fall. It never did. I still wonder why Daddy did not confront me. He probably thought that I had suffered enough to justify my behavior. Or, did he, after years of working mules, simply understand and agree with my words and actions?

A good friend of mine once asked, "Where did you get your outstanding tolerance and patience with people?" I suppose it came from working mules.

Mules may not have caused cussing, but they surely contributed to the advancement of the artful use of profanity.

Idle Hands . . .

My dad was born to work—and I mean *work really hard*—at manual labor. He lived by the old adage, "Idle hands are the devil's workshop." My grandfather died before I was born, but somehow I came to believe that he passed on an overkill of work ethic to my father. This was especially true when it came to "lift that barge, tote that bale" kind of work. I believe my father inherited and used up the manual-labor component of our heritage, leaving none for me. I could ignore the barge and take a nap on the bale. I noticed that the men with the clean clothes and callous-free hands seemed to have the money. So at an early age, I decided that farming was not my bag. I also possessed a curiosity for what it would be like to do some of that "devil's workshop" stuff. I loved and respected my father so much that I wanted to please him, so I worked alongside him as if I were born to toil.

Once, my dad, my three sisters, and I were working in the tobacco field, hoeing the few blades of grass that were scattered about. My sisters and I thought this to be totally unnecessary, but Dad would be embarrassed to have any visible vegetation in the field other than tobacco. Then it started to rain. My sisters and I began to complain. "Daddy, can we stop? It is raining."

Dad surveyed the sky and said, "It is not raining hard enough to stop yet."

Soon the rain was coming down in buckets, and we were soaked. Again we pleaded, "Can we stop now?"

Dad looked to the sky and said, "We are already wet now, so we may as well keep working." Until this day I have not sorted out the rationale in that one.

Working so closely together on the farm gave my dad many opportunities to pass wisdom on to us kids. We hauled the cured tobacco from the curing barn to the pack house for storage until we were ready to sell it in the fall. The tobacco was packed on a trailer and pulled by tractor to the pack house. My job was to sit on a small space at the back of the trailer and watch for any tobacco leaves that might fall off. I would then jump off, run back, pick up the fallen leaves, and deliver them back to the trailer. My dad used the eyes in the back of his head to monitor my performance. Once, when he was hauling a load of tobacco, a little wind whipped

up and a few leaves fell off. It was very near noon, dinnertime on the farm. I was tired and hungry, so I ignored the fallen leaves. Abruptly, my dad stopped the tractor, turned to me, and said, "LaVerne, get those leaves."

In a whining voice I said, "Daddy, they ain't worth picking up."

Dad cut the tractor engine off, swiveled the seat around, stared that soulful stare that he was good at, and asked, "LaVerne, you tell me, how many leaves would have to fall off before they would be worth picking up?"

Through the years I have thought often of that lesson as I have noticed the abandonment of an ethical rule here and a moral code there. How many must fall off the wagon before we pause and pick them up?

Sibling Camaraderie

Much has been said and written in our culture about sibling rivalry. One would think that children in the same family would never really get along. When I think of growing up with three sisters and no brothers, I have a different take on our childhood together. I think more about the camaraderie we shared. Although we did fight both verbally and physically, we had a wonderful love for and strong bonds with each other.

Being outnumbered by girls three to one, I do see (looking back over my life) that I have carried some effeminate characteristics with me. I played house with dolls and made corn-shuck dolls alongside my sisters. I played predominately girls' games like hopscotch, jack rocks (jacks), jump rope, and such. I would often assert my masculinity and demand to be the mailman if playing house. That gave me the opportunity to bring in some boy stuff. For example, I could chase down highwaymen who were attempting to steal the mail. Playing with my sisters always seemed to come down to my having to be a tea-party kind of guy. Anyway, go on the Internet and see what a big deal corn-shuck doll making and collecting is today for both men and women.

When I started school and began building buddy relationships with boys, I had to shift gears and catch up on how to play boy stuff. This training came naturally and quickly. I became somewhat of a leader among my Bend buddies, as you may have surmised after reading about our antics, pranks, and adventures in the Bend in my other stories.

Throughout our growing-up years, I developed a uniquely different relationship with each of my sisters. These unique relationships live in my mind even today.

Betty Jean was three years older than I. Since girls develop physically and emotionally faster than boys, the age difference between us was more pronounced. Betty Jean bossed me around and in our fights got the better of me. She was skilled at having Mama believe that I was at fault in every instance. This situation was resolved when I was about nine years old. Elaine was a little over six and Brenda was a toddler. When Mama and Daddy went to Danville one day and left twelve-year-old Betty Jean in charge, she and I got into a fight. I allowed years of resentment toward her to fly loose. I won the fight. I was expecting all hell to come down on me

when our parents returned. Mama asked, "Betty Jean, how did you children behave while we were gone?" Betty Jean smiled and said, "Everyone did just fine." From that day forward Betty Jean and I never physically fought again, although we did have some verbal fights from time to time. I even felt her love for me, and my resentment toward her disappeared completely.

Betty Jean died way too young, at fifty-seven years old, from cancer. The cancer started in her breast and metastasized to her bones. Her illness came in a time when I had considerable freedom and could take Mama to visit her often. Elaine and Brenda also visited her frequently. Lucille and I made arrangements with a local florist to bring her flowers weekly for the last year of her life. I will never forget how much she looked forward to those flowers.

Two events stand out in my memory when I think of Betty Jean.

Once after Betty Jean and I had our momentous fight, a much larger boy was getting the best of me in a fight. Suddenly Betty Jean appeared out of nowhere and flew into a "hell hath no fury like a woman"—you know the rest of the story. She beat that boy into total submission.

She made him say, "I'm sorry," and then she came and put her arm around me and asked if I was okay. She walked away as if her actions had been a piece of cake. My love for her at that moment rang the bell.

Mama and I visited Betty Jean about two weeks before she died. She was still able to go to her favorite restaurant for lunch, although she had to be carried in a wheelchair. Her body had shrunk to childlike size. She wouldn't wear a wig. She wore a turban. As I was pushing her into the restaurant, she looked up at Mama and me with a big, beautiful, broad smile and said, "This has been the best year of my life."

Betty Jean had a strong faith in God and believed that a better life awaited her. Thank you, Betty Jean. Because of you I have less fear of death.

I remember vividly the night Elaine was born. Old Dr. Dillard came to deliver her at home as was the practice in those days. Elaine was born prematurely at seven months. I was three years and eleven days old when she was born. I was lying in a baby bed covered with a bedsheet in my parents' bedroom when she was born. I suppose that everyone thought, *What would a three-year-old child remember about this event?* Well, remember I did. I could hear the consternation in their voices and Mama crying and asking, "Will she die?" I remember Mama, Daddy, and old Dr. Dillard praying for Elaine's life and my sensing the anxiousness in the room.

Describing the night to Mama some years later, I learned that Elaine weighed only two pounds at birth and was bedded in a shoebox. Mama and Daddy's love, attention, and prayers saved my dear sister Elaine's life. This was a miracle considering her birth date was February 28, 1940.

That experience created an unbreakable bond between Elaine and me. We never physically fought. The bond between us has endured.

I never told you my following thoughts before, Elaine. When I was diagnosed with a blinding disease, I thought, *Elaine survived much worse odds. We Thorntons must have strong survival instincts.*

The thing I remember most about growing up with Elaine was her ability to mimic people. In our

area there lived a saintly man whom I remember only as Rev. Travis. Rev. Travis stood ready to fill any empty pulpit in any church at any time that it was vacant for any reason. Rev. Travis was a tall, skinny man with a shock of white hair. He looked like a man who, as a line in some country song says, had been too long in the sun, too long in the rain, and too long close up to pain. He wore one black suit, one narrow black tie, and an outdated black derby hat. Even with his necktie pulled snugly around his collar, you could put a full hand in the space between his neck and his shirt collar. He had a huge Adam's apple that moved up and down when he spoke. Rev. Travis had no formal education and had a limited vocabulary. He probably never preached a really profound sermon, but he never preached a sermon that was less than sincere and from the heart. His faithfulness alone inspired people.

Elaine mimicked Rev. Travis to perfection. We would set up a pulpit, entrap as many neighbor kids as possible, and pretend to have an old-fashioned revival complete with funeral home fans and a collection plate, albeit no one ever put money in the plate. I would introduce Elaine as our visiting minister. I would say, "Tonight we have with us the extremely reverent, holy man of God, teacher of the gospel, and every man's friend, Preacher Travis." Elaine would then

stand on the pulpit, usually a stump, and deliver a really good sermon complete with all of Rev. Travis's words and gestures.

At the end of one of her best sermons, Elaine turned her back to us in the congregation and made a bow to the make-believe choir. As she bent over, there was a very visible hole in her panties. The congregation broke up with laughter, and the service ended abruptly.

Elaine and I still share growing-up stories when we get together.

Brenda, who was born six years after me, was small and frail in her early years, but she was very athletic. Working hard on the farm had made me quite strong. Brenda and I used her athletic ability and agility plus my strength to build an acrobatic duo. The acrobatic activities increased her strength also. We worked out a routine of several acts and would often entertain the family. One of the routines went as follows: I would lie on my back on the ground with my knees bent. Brenda would stand on my knees with her hands on my shoulders and slowly move into a handstand. I would then slowly rise to a standing position. Once when doing this act, Brenda fell and either broke her wrist or severely sprained it. I felt terrible for days, but once Brenda healed, we went back to our acts and soon developed even more skilled performances. Our most impressive skit was to have me lie on my back with knees bent. Brenda would take a running start, place her hands on my knees, and initiate a somersault. I would catch her shoulders just as her body was near vertical and thrust her upward in a flipping motion. Brenda would do a complete flip, landing on her feet. We were smart enough in perfecting this act to provide padding on the landing spot. We were successful enough occasionally to get a double flip.

Being the last or youngest child in the family can be tough. The youngest child follows kids who have developed skills at teasing and kidding. In general, the older children have learned to dish it out as well as take it. This leaves the youngest one vulnerable. When Brenda was about seven years old, Betty Jean, Elaine, and I told Brenda that Mama and Daddy planned to have the three of us but that she was just an accident. Brenda really took it seriously and was terribly hurt. I think her feelings were healed considerably when Mama punished the three of us harshly and gave Brenda special privileges for a few days.

Brenda married a man who joined and remained in the U.S. Navy for about ten years. They lived far from the rest of the family for all those years in places like the Philippines, Spain, and Rhode Island. I learned that if all parties don't work at it, geography can lessen family ties. Our family did work at it, and we have been successful in maintaining the strong family bonds that were built during our formative years while growing up in the Bend.

Brenda grew up to be very skilled and has had success in a number of diversified careers. Her heart is so big and her sensitivity to other people's problems is so keen that she tends to carry the burdens of others on her own shoulders. With the tendency of people today to succumb to the "Me first" society in which we live, that ain't a bad thing. If I ever need to walk through the valley of the shadow of death, I would like to have Brenda beside me holding my hand and giving me her loving support.

Growing up with three sisters and no brothers, I have always been aware of the discrimination that girls and women have faced in society, especially in the era in which we grew up.

Back in 1987, I was in a business meeting in Germany. The company that we were visiting manufactured specialty equipment for use in flour mills. An Englishman and I were there to evaluate the adaptability of one of their machines to our powered coal fuel systems. The meeting started promptly at eight o'clock in the morning. Germans tend to be prompt even if they have nothing to do. At precisely ten o'clock one of the Germans said that he would have his girls bring us coffee and cakes. The old feelings of discrimination simmering in my soul surfaced, and I felt empathy for the woman who brought in coffee and cakes to us chauvinistic men. It had been years since I had experienced things like that in our country.

I honestly believe that the many imperfections that I have today are fewer and less harmful to other people because of the sibling camaraderie that I shared with Betty Jean, Elaine, and Brenda while growing up in the bend of the Dan River.

Taught by Adages and Proverbs

My grandmother, Shotgun Essie, knew every proverb and adage known to mankind. She didn't just quote them but applied them to events and circumstances as a way to teach. She especially loved teaching me because I would ask endless questions about the meaning of those old sayings. Many people my age had similar experiences. Lucille and I were having dinner with a doctor friend and his wife one evening. Somewhere in the conversation the husband said, "As my old granny used to say, 'Two birds in a bush are better than nine stitches in time.'" We laughed out loud and hard at that one. After his wife straightened him out, we started to discuss old adages such as, "A stitch in time saves nine," "You can lead a horse to water, but you can't make him drink," "A rolling stone gathers no moss," and so on. That night before going to sleep, I reflected on all the old proverbs and adages that my grandmother taught me.

Once, when I was staying overnight with Granny, she noticed a small rip in my overalls—the white ones that earned me the nickname "Whistle Britches." She said, "Son, take your overalls off and let me mend that tear; 'A stitch in time saves nine.'" I asked her all manner of questions. What is a stitch? Would it take nine stitches? Granny took time to explain how this expression applied to life. She explained that if you have a tear in a friendship, mend it immediately or it will get worse and may go beyond repair. I still practice that lesson today.

Putting this adage into practice, however, can backfire. A woman in our church really insulted me unfairly one time. To prevent this from developing into a fractured relationship, I called on her and told her that I was sorry for the misunderstanding that had happened between us. She smiled and said, "Not to worry, I have already forgiven you." The meaning was lost to her but the friendship survived.

Granny did not have to compete with TV and video games. As stated previously, I am now seventy-two years of age. I don't remember what I saw on TV last night, but I do remember every detail of those lessons my grandmother taught me and the patience she had with her little grandboy.

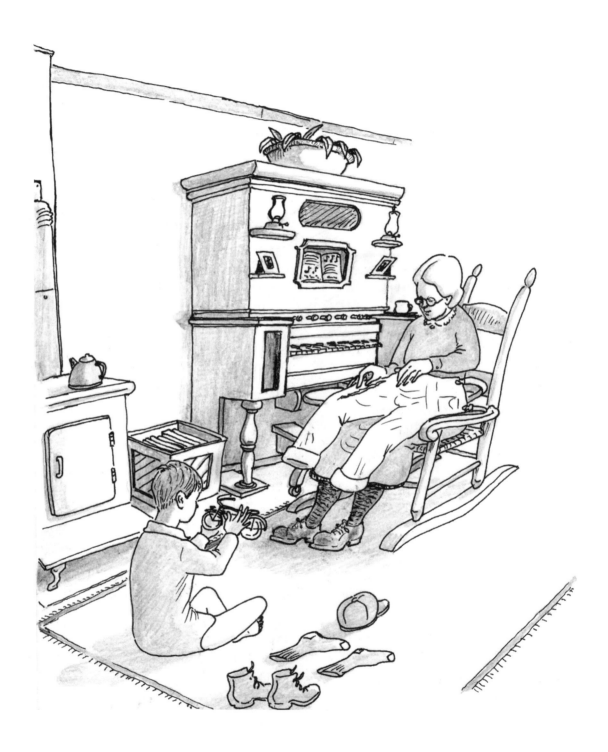

Just before my twenty-eighth birthday, Lucille noticed that I was squinting at everything I looked at and insisted that I go for an eye exam. I went to an older optometrist in Sanford, North Carolina. He took an especially long time examining me before telling me, "You have a condition called keratoconus. The disease has already caused you to be almost legally blind. The condition is not curable and will result in total blindness." We had just moved into the first home that we built. Our daughter LaVisa was three years old, and our son Perry was an infant. I sang all the way home thinking that I could possibly become a blind singer. This thought was abandoned as I listened to my monotone voice. No words could express the dread of having to tell Lucille and the fear of facing life as a blind person.

That night while lying in bed thinking, I remembered my grandmother once telling me, "If the wolf comes to your door, jerk the little rascal inside and make him into a foot warmer!" The wolf wasn't at our door yet, but we could hear him howling in the distance. Instead of thinking of how one applies for welfare, I started to think about gathering the things needed to make a foot warmer. About a month later I went to a younger doctor and learned that hard contact lenses could keep me seeing for awhile, but should not be worn more than four hours per day. This time limit was impossible for me to keep with my job responsibilities and a family to feed, so I wore the lenses all day every day, living with constant pain. The person who invented contact lenses was an ophthalmologist who had my disease. Technology and twelve eye surgeries have preserved my eyesight thus far. Every time I get close to losing my vision, a new technology keeps me seeing. It may sound strange because the battle isn't over yet, but facing blindness has caused a series of positive happenings in my life. I never got that foot warmer made.

In 1978 at age forty-one, I worked for a company that manufactured vitrified clay, sanitary sewer pipe. I had at that time been with the company nineteen years. I had received nine promotions during those years and at the time was vice president of operations responsible for two manufacturing plants, one in North Carolina and one in Pennsylvania. I was also responsible for the trucking operation as well as engineering research and development. I felt on top of the world.

Right after negotiating a contract with the steelworkers union in the Pennsylvania plant, for which I received praise from the company president, I was summoned to the company headquarters in Greensboro, North Carolina. I was so naïve that I truly believed that I was going to be named president of the company. I drove the fifty miles to Greensboro in record time. I daydreamed about my big raise and my new Cadillac or Mercedes company car. I got a little peeved near Siler City thinking, *I sure hope I don't get gray leather like my boss's car*. I preferred a tan interior.

The minute I walked into my boss's office, I sensed that something was wrong. After praising me for all my contributions over the nineteen years I had been with the company, he said, "LaVerne, I think you need to change careers. I believe you are in over your head. I am asking you for your resignation." He added, "I had planned to ask you for your resignation last year, but your dad died and your wife was diagnosed with rheumatoid arthritis." I immediately thought how cruel it was for him to keep me around knowing all those things.

He gave me severance pay and my company car so I didn't have to hitchhike home. The drive home was worse than awful. It started to rain, and at one point I stopped under a bridge and wept. I must have driven two hundred miles to get home fifty miles away. I rehearsed over and over what I would tell Lucille. She was just getting over what the doctors call a "rheumatoid episode." LaVisa was finishing high school that spring and planned to go to college. Perry was completing the ninth grade. Lucille took the news very well and assured me that things would work out; I was not so sure.

I was awake late into the night when I thought of something my grandmother told me once when I was in a down mood. She said, "If you ever get run out of town, strut like you are leading a parade!" I had just been run out of town. I went to sleep and awakened the next day strutting. I decided to go out on my own as a consulting engineer. With a few phone calls and a bit of networking, I had a good contract with a Fortune 500 company within three days. I was under contract to put together an alternative energy project utilizing combustible biomass for industrial fuel. This led to the formation of a successful engineering and construction company with two other men. I have never drawn a paycheck from anyone but myself since that fateful day in Greensboro, North Carolina.

The company that fired me went out of business about five years after I left. In spite of what happened to me, I was pained by that company closing. I had left a bunch of great people there and many fond memories.

I would often walk with my friend of nineteen years, Dave Watson. Early one cold morning in November, we were discussing the subject of aging. Dave is nine years older than I and one of my inspirations. I said, "Dave, when I was young, I had pretty blue eyes and wavy black hair. My eyes have gone bad; my hair has turned white and turned loose. My spine is deteriorating, causing me to lose three and one-half inches in height." We both laughed and I added, "One thing I can boast about, though; I have a really good, strong heart." On January 28 of the following year, I was having quintuple bypass surgery at Duke Hospital in Durham, North Carolina. As I lay on a gurney waiting to be taken into surgery, I asked Granny for an appropriate adage for the occasion. I could hear Granny say only this, "Pride goeth before a fall." I made a remarkable recovery. Granny knew that I would. She would be ashamed of me if I didn't.

These stories are not told in any way to boast, but to illustrate how simple lessons learned from an uneducated granny armed with wisdom, proverbs, and corny adages taught one little boy how to get through tough times in the Bend and taught one imperfect man how to get through tough times in life.

Thank you, sweet Shotgun Essie; you taught me well. I love you still. I will stay tuned.

As the Twig Is Bent, So Grows the Tree

All the mischief I was involved in while growing up would appear to be basic training for a life as a ne'er-do-well or for a life of crime. It's a truth that we Bend boys pushed the envelope on devilment and mischief that sometimes bordered on crime. Perhaps if we had been exposed to all the choices that confront teenagers today, some of us would have pursued lives of crime. We did live in an era influenced by Chicago mobsters, John Dillinger, Baby Face Nelson, and the likes. They were often portrayed as folk heroes or modern-day Robin Hoods. One boy in our group wanted to emulate the local bootlegger who had a fast car and a reputation for evading the law.

As I grew up, there was—by society's standards—a less fascinating story being written, although a more important one. That story was about my parents, my maternal Granny Essie, and the overwhelmingly positive influences that they had on the kind of person who I eventually became. My parents lived by strict moral and ethical codes, influenced by their church-centered lives and their own upbringings. My parents instilled in Betty Jean, Elaine, Brenda, and me a strong work ethic, a strict moral code, and an especially strong respect for human, animal, and plant life. We were taught scripture from the King James Version of the Bible, such as Psalm 24:1: "The earth is the Lord's, and the fullness thereof; the world, and they that dwell therein," and Psalm 1:3, that the Godly man "shall be like a tree planted by the rivers of water, that bringeth forth his fruit in his season; his leaf also shall not wither; and whatsoever he doeth shall prosper."

We were taught that we were born into this life as unfinished human beings and that through hard work and right living we could have some control over our own destinies and prosperity. Though we were poor, we were taught to share with and help others in need. These scriptures and principles have remained strong aspects of my character throughout my life.

One of Daddy's favorite stories illustrated how to be a good custodian of the earth. I have told this story over and over to others during my lifetime. I will attempt to tell it here. One time a minister took over a new church in a farming community. He and his family got settled in on a Wednesday. He decided to drive around the area and visit some of his parishioners. With the church roll book in hand, he started out. When he saw a name on a mailbox that matched

one of his church member's names, he would stop and introduce himself. After several stops he came upon a really pretty farm. There was a long driveway leading to a beautiful white farmhouse. On each side of the driveway was a lush, green pasture inhabited with romping horses and grazing cattle. A crisp red barn with white trim stood only one hundred feet away from the house. The minister stopped at the side yard of the house and got out as the farmer drove up in his tractor. The minister stepped forward and introduced himself. After a brief "How do you do?" and "Isn't it a nice day?" type of conversation, the minister surveyed the pastoral scene and exclaimed, "My, my, this is a beautiful farm you and the Lord have here." The farmer spat his tobacco juice and replied, "You should have seen it when the Lord had it by hisself." That farmer had been a good custodian of God's earth. He knew that God had given him stewardship over that land and that his own hard work was required to make that land into a beautiful farm. I am reminded daily that I am just a steward while here on God's earth.

While Shotgun Essie would appear in my stories to be complicit in some of our mischief, she would counsel me when it appeared to her that we had or were about to cross the line of a moral or ethical code. I think Granny was wise enough to believe that if we confided in each other, she would have a better opportunity to train me in the right ways.

Granny had a battery radio with two knobs, one being a combination on/off/volume knob. The second knob was used to tune into three stations that we could receive on a good day. The radio was generally useless at night. This lack of radio "noise" left a few simple games and conversation as our nightly activities. My warmest memories of those nights are when Granny would lie across the bed while I lay beside her. Granny loved to tell me once-upon-a-time stories while I scratched her back. As I grew older, those conversations grew more serious. One time I told her about a boy with whom I was playing and some activity that we were planning. Granny gently and lovingly warned me by saying, "Be careful with that boy and don't be influenced by him. I hear some bad things about him." She then read appropriate scripture from Genesis 3. Granny explained that sin came on earth when Eve was influenced by the serpent and Adam was influenced by Eve, and they both did what God had forbidden. Granny told me that I was wise beyond my years and that I should be the influencer and not the one being influenced in my relationship with that boy. She then pulled up some old proverbs and adages: "A person is known by the company he keeps," and "Birds of a feather will flock together." Then there was my favorite one of all: "Lie down with dogs, and you may get up with fleas." I knew what dogs with fleas were like, and I wanted no part of them. Granny could paint such a vivid picture with her explanations of that adage that I would sometimes itch and start scratching. These were lessons from scripture and adages that have guided my life in my relationships with others.

The one old adage that Granny never quoted to me was, "As the twig is bent, so grows the tree." I suppose that Granny thought if she taught me that one, I would see into her primary purpose of sharing her wisdom with me. That purpose was to bend the tender twig that I was during those times in the right directions so that I would grow into the tree, "planted by the rivers of water," that God meant for me to be.

As I got into my late teens, my parents' examples and Granny's teachings caused my character to develop more and more around Daddy's and Mama's exemplary lives and Granny's diligent efforts.

Sweet Granny Essie, because you kept bending the twig in the right directions, I don't have fleas. I flock with wonderful birds. I am proud to be known by the company I keep. Thank you!

As the twig is bent…

So grows the tree.

Walk in 'e Moon

I was no doubt, as a child, a mama's boy.

Mama had rheumatic fever as she was birthing me. Rheumatic fever can leave a person with a heart murmur, even if that person is strong and in good health when contracting the disease. With the burden placed on a woman's body while giving birth, the presence of rheumatic fever has an even more devastating effect. As a result of the disease, Mama developed a very severe heart murmur and remained in poor health for the rest of her life. Eventually, the murmur led to her death from congestive heart failure in 1997 at the age of eighty-six. Even with her condition, Mama lived the life of a farmer's wife with all the hard work that is associated with that life.

Less was known about her condition back then, and very few drugs were available for treatment. Mama lived far longer than was expected. As she grew older, better treatment became available, and Mama understood her condition better. A combination of managing her condition, proper exercise, using more effective drugs, and cutting down on hard work extended her life. I think her amazing positive attitude and her outlook on life were the major contributors to a longer and happier life.

In spite of her condition, Mama went on to have two more children after me. She told me later that she had no regrets. She said, "Each of you children was worth dying for."

I feel that even at a young age, I always knew Mama almost died and that her poor health was a result of my birth. However I became aware of that fact, it created a bond between Mama and me that lasted a lifetime for her and will also for me. I felt a need to help her, as I was able, with her hard work. My feeling that my birth almost killed Mama was confirmed by one of her sisters. I was visiting my cousin when I was about ten years old, and for some reason my aunt said, "Sister almost died when you were born." All my life I vowed that someday I would help make things up to Mama.

If Mama went to the garden to pick peas, dig potatoes, or perform any of her gardening chores, I would stop playing and go with her to help. These garden trips provided an

opportunity to talk with Mama about life, nature, and all sorts of things. I truly believe that my basic philosophy of life came from those garden trips with Mama. Our talks had an effect on my life that will be with me forever. I often wonder how many valuable lessons about life are missed by kids who have iPods plugged into their ears or because Mama is on the computer.

When I was fifty-two, my partners and I sold our engineering and construction company. Although I dabbled in business after that, I remained semiretired for the next ten years. Those years coincided with the last ten years of Mama's life. I spent a considerable amount of this time becoming really good friends with Mama. I would visit her and stay overnight about every two weeks. I would take her on short trips and visit friends and relatives. We would eat out every meal.

On one of my visits I got up the nerve to tell Mama about my thinking that my birth was responsible for her poor health. She looked at me with a most loving look and assured me that having me as a son had made her life so rich that nothing could have happened to her that would diminish my value to her. The subject never came up again. Thank you, Mama.

On these visits we talked as two adult friends would talk. We did a good deal of reminiscing about our life on the farm. Mama and I shared story after story during these visits. Mama told me two stories about our special bond that she would never forget.

Mama expected me to perform any chores that the girls did and vice versa. One day when I was around eleven, Mama assigned me the task of hanging out the wash. A few days later we went to Danville, and as usual I wandered around town while Mama took my sisters shopping for clothes. There were a few of the girls' clothes that Mama did not sew herself. Mama said that I returned with a bag from the Belk Leggett store. That was not unusual for me because I would often use money that I had earned working for other tobacco farmers to buy odds and ends for myself.

When we got home, Mama said that when I saw her alone, I brought her that bag and said, "Mama, when I was hanging out the wash last week, I saw that your underwear had holes in them so I bought you some new ones."

Mama said, "I don't remember if I thanked you properly at the time because I was so choked up that I had to be alone and have a good cry." She wondered aloud how I had managed that purchase in a day when women's underwear was referred to as "unmentionables."

I replied, "Mama, the way you raised me, I really didn't know that there was anything so strange about a little boy buying his mama some underwear. I bought them from a woman about your size." I had forgotten that story until Mama jogged my memory. This story reminded me of the sacrifices most mothers make to provide for their children. A good mother will wear rags, if necessary, to provide good clothes for her children.

Mama and I talked about our love of walking on paths much traveled at night in the moonlight. Mama said that at about three years old I had a fascination with nature, particularly the moon and stars. Very often after she had finished her after-supper chores, I would ease up and tug at her skirt and say, "Mama, let's walk in 'e moon."

Mama said, "I loved those walks; you would talk on and on about God, nature, and many other things. I called you my little philosopher."

Mama said that I told her once while walking in 'e moon, "Mama, when I get grown, you won't have to work so hard."

Mama and I got to walk in the moonlight several times again; except those times, I held her hand in support of her as she once did me. A stroke left her feeble, but it did not affect her indomitable spirit or her habit of getting so tickled at things that she would wet herself laughing.

Sometimes when I am feeling weary or bored or in some way find the present disturbing, I will take a deep breath, close my eyes, and take a "walk in 'e moon" with Mama.